Henry Edward Krehbiel

Music and Manners in the classical Period

Henry Edward Krehbiel

Music and Manners in the classical Period

ISBN/EAN: 9783337060145

Printed in Europe, USA, Canada, Australia, Japan

Cover: Foto ©ninafisch / pixelio.de

More available books at **www.hansebooks.com**

MUSIC AND MANNERS

IN THE CLASSICAL PERIOD

ESSAYS

BY

HENRY EDWARD KREHBIEL

AUTHOR OF "HOW TO LISTEN TO MUSIC," "STUDIES IN THE
WAGNERIAN DRAMA," "NOTES ON THE CULTIVATION
OF CHORAL MUSIC," "THE PHILHARMONIC
SOCIETY OF NEW YORK," ETC.

NEW YORK
CHARLES SCRIBNER'S SONS
1898

TO
SIR GEORGE GROVE, C.B.

CONTENTS

A POET'S MUSIC

		PAGE
I.	Gray's Musical Collection	3
II.	The Poet's Taste	15
III.	Last Century Singers	40

HAYDN IN LONDON

| I. | His Note Book | 57 |
| II. | His English Love | 95 |

A MOZART CENTENARY

I.	Social and Artistic Salzburg	115
II.	The Composer's Domestic Life	128
III.	Music at the Festival	142
IV.	Da Ponte in New York	159

BEETHOVEN AND HIS BIOGRAPHER

| I. | Alexander Wheelock Thayer | 191 |
| II. | The Beethoven Museum at Bonn | 212 |

REFLECTIONS IN WEIMAR

The Influence of Goethe and Liszt — 243

INDEX 265

A POET'S MUSIC

I
GRAY'S MUSICAL COLLECTION

But the two most interesting items of the catalogue are yet unmentioned. One is the laborious collection of Manuscript Music that Gray compiled in Italy while frivolous Horace Walpole was eating iced fruits in a domino to the sound of a guitar. Zamperelli, Pergolesi, Arrigoni, Galuppi — he had ransacked them all, noting the school of the composer and the source of the piece selected — copying out religiously even the "Regole per l'Accompagnamento."

It is thus that Austin Dobson alludes, in one of his "Eighteenth Century Vignettes," to a portion of the library of the author of the "Elegy written in a Country Churchyard." He is writing with a catalogue of a sale of the poet's library, which took place in 1851, as his guide. The second of the "two most interesting items" was an interleaved copy of the "Systema Naturæ," by Linnæus, which Mr. Ruskin exhibited at Cambridge in 1885, "covered as to their margins and added pages with wonderful minute notes in Latin, and illustrated by Gray himself with delicately finished pen-and-ink drawings of birds and insects." This Mr. Dobson had seen when he wrote his vignette entitled "Gray's Library," but on the precious collection of music he never laid his eyes; nor does he know what became of it. In 1887 the "New York Tribune" contributed a chapter to its history telling how at a sale of some of the books of Charles W. Frederickson (since dead) in 1886 the auctioneer, Mr. Bangs, had bought the musical manuscripts himself and presented them to Mrs. C. M. Raymond — she that music lovers in the United States and Great Britain knew and loved as Annie Louise Cary. From Mrs. Raymond's hands they passed into those of their present owner, and they are this moment smiling down upon the writer from one of his bookshelves.[1] I purpose to draw a chapter or two of musical history from the manuscripts presently, and to this end occupy myself first with a description of the nine volumes before me.

The volumes are each twelve inches long

---

[1] A tenth volume, made up of fragments evidently found in Gray's desk after his death, seems to have been overlooked by Mr. Bangs. It was sold in May, 1897, for seventy dollars.

and nine inches wide and vary in thickness, containing on an average two hundred sheets of extremely heavy hand-made paper. The edges are untrimmed. The sheets are bound stoutly in hogskin covers, most of which are lettered on the back and front in the handwriting of the poet. The music has been copied as a rule in a bold style by a professional copyist, but Gray has added some airs, besides many notes, and provided each of the volumes with a table of contents most beautifully and daintily written. The music consists almost exclusively of operatic airs from the composers who were the chief glory of the Italian schools of the eighteenth century. Of them more anon. The music is in score — that is, the full orchestral part is written out as well as the vocal; but inasmuch as the operatic band of the early part of the eighteenth century (the collection was made in 1740) seldom consisted of more than the stringed instruments, five or six staves suffice to contain the music. Noteworthy exceptions to this rule will be mentioned in the detailed description of the volumes. Gray's annotations are concerned with the titles of the operas from which the airs were taken, the names of the dramatic personages who sang them, and the names of singers whom he had heard in the operas or who had identified themselves in some particular manner with the music. This point cannot be determined, though the circumstance that occasionally a date, and sometimes also the name of a city, is added indicates that he intended by the notes to preserve a record of individual enjoyments.

Commenting on the care with which Gray's books have been preserved by their later possessors, Mr. Dobson says: "Many of the Note-Books were cushioned on velvet in special cases, while the more precious manuscripts had been skilfully inlaid and bound in olive morocco with leather joints and linings of crimson silk." The musical manuscripts belong to those thus piously preserved. Each volume rests in an elegant wooden case covered with purple morocco and lined with cushions of black silk velvet. These cases are each shaped like a book, tooled and lettered uniformly:

GRAY'S MUSICAL COLLECTION

Below these panels follow the names of the composers represented in the different volumes.

The history of the collection since Gray's death in 1771 lies before us in a tolerably clear and complete record. By his will he gave to the Rev. William Mason all his " books, manuscripts, coins, music, printed or written, and papers of all kinds, to preserve or destroy at his own discretion." This was the Rev. William Mason who published a memoir of the poet in connection with an edition of his works in 1775. He was precentor of York Cathedral, and in 1782 published " A Copious Collection of those Portions of the Psalms of David, Bible and Liturgy which have been set to Music and sung as Anthems in the Cathedral and Collegiate Churches of England." Mason kept the music till he died and bequeathed it along with the rest of the library "to the poet's friend, Stonehewer," says Mr. Dobson. The name of this gentleman and the names of his immediate successors in the ownership of the manuscripts appear in lead-pencil writing several times in the volumes. One memorandum reads as follows : " Richard Stonehewer (or Stenhewer) Esqr., Curzon-st., London "; another, " Richard Bright, Esq., Skeffington Hall, 1818 "; another, " E. Bright,

A POET'S MUSIC

May 22d, 1819"; still another, "Revd. John Bright." Mr. Bright of Skeffington Hall was a relative of Mr. Stonehewer (if that name be correct), and got the library from him. It remained in the Bright family till 1845, when it was first dispersed by public sale. There were sales of portions of Gray's library in 1845, 1847, 1851 and 1854, the music forming a part of the sale of 1851. Mr. Frederickson bought it in England, but whether at the sale of 1851 or not I cannot say.

Here follows a detailed description of the nine volumes in question, the volumes being numbered for convenience' sake:

I. Inscribed by Gray on the cover: "Arie del Sigr. G. Adolfo Hasse detto Il Sassone. Firenze, 1740." Contains twenty-five airs from the operas "Alessandro nell' Indie," "La Clemenza di Tito," "Demetrio," "Issipile," "Artaserse" and "Siroë." The singers mentioned are Carestini, Faustina, Farinelli (whom, save once, Gray uniformly calls Farinello) and Tesi.

II. Not inscribed or indexed, but containing autograph notes by Gray. The contents are twenty arias, two duets and one trio from "Catone," "Tito," "Issipile," "Artaserse" and "Siroë"—all by Hasse. Two of the airs are in Gray's handwriting.

GRAY'S MUSICAL COLLECTION

III. Gray's inscription on cover: "Arie del Sigr. Leonardo Vinci, Napoletano. Firenze, 1740." Contains twenty-five airs and one duet from the operas "Catone," "Alessandro," "Semiramide," "Demofoonte," "Andromaca" and "Artaserse." Also a solo cantata, by Vinci, and the following pieces copied by Gray: a cantata for solo voice by Pergolese; a "Toccata per il Cembalo del Sassone" followed by two minuets; three arias from Vinci's "Artaserse" and one from Latilla's "Siroë" dated "Roma, 1740"; two arias from unmentioned operas by Hasse and Giaii; five instrumental pieces — a minuet by Giacomelli ("Roma"), another minuet by Hasse (called here, as was the custom in Italy, *Il Sassone*, i. e., "The Saxon"); an arietta from an overture by David Perez, followed by a minuet, and an arietta from "Siroë" by Latilla, dated "Roma, 1740." In all there are forty-four pages in Gray's handwriting. The singers mentioned are Farfallino, Carestini, Farinelli, Faustina, Senesino and Cuzzoni. In three of the arias the strings are supplemented with trumpets, and one has two horns and oboes besides two trumpets.

IV. A volume uninscribed by Gray, but marked "Vinci" on the back. It is devoted wholly to a cantata, which is one of the most interesting compositions in the collection. Strangely enough, though Gray has made an index of all the musical numbers and added the names of the *dramatis personæ* he has neglected to give the name of the work. This could only be determined by its text, aided by historical research. These disclose that it is the cantata entitled " La Contesa de' Numi," which Vinci composed in 1729, at the command of the Marquis de Polignac, then French Ambassador at Rome, to celebrate the birthday of the Dauphin Louis, son of Louis XV, and father of Louis XVI. The words are by Metastasio. The characters are *Jove, Apollo, Mars, Astræa, Peace* and *Fortune*. The cantata is in two parts, each containing seven vocal numbers, six solos and a concluding *Coro grande*, which (as was the case in the operas of the period) is an *ensemble* in which all the solo characters join. The first part is preceded by an overture, which Gray describes as "*à ten parti*," the ten parts being two violins, two trumpets, two trombe da caccia, two oboes, bassoon and double bass — the last two in unison. The piece consists of a stately minuet, followed by a rapid movement in common time. The instrumental introduction to the second part Gray calls "Simfonia." It is a minuet followed by a brief intermezzo for strings alone in common time, after which the minuet is repeated. In their tripartite form the pieces suggest the overture form as fixed by Lully. In one of the numbers of the second part, an extremely florid air, the orchestra consists of two trombe da caccia, two flutes (called *traversieri*), violins, viola, bassoon and bass, and there is a general direction that the cembalo (harpsichord) be not used. The reason for this is plain, for the number has an *obbligato* part for the *salterio*, that is, the dulcimer, an instrument which we meet with now only in the bands of the Hungarian gypsies.

V. A volume of excerpts from the compositions of Leonardo Leo. No external inscription, but a full table of contents in Gray's handwriting. Leo being as great a composer of church music as of operas, the book begins with four motets for solo voice and orchestra. Then there are fourteen airs from " Achille," " Ciro Riconosciuto," " Olimpiade " and " Artaserse," and two duets from " Olimpiade." The singers mentioned are La Strada, Giziello (whom Gray calls " Egiziello "), Tesi and Carestini. An aria sung by La Strada in " Achille " is dated " 1739, Turino."

VI. A volume containing twenty arias and

two duets by Michele Fini from "Issipile," "Didone," "Siroë," "Alessandro," "Tito Manlio," "Rodelinda," "Farnace" and "Temistocle." The singers mentioned are Tesi, Turcotti, Lo Scalzi and Cuzzoni. Two airs of Tesi's are marked "Pisa" in Gray's handwriting, and a duet from "Tito Manlio" is inscribed "Cant: dalla Cuzzoni e La Scalzi, Bologna." A duet from "Rodelinda" is dated "Livorno." The book begins with the "Regole per l'Accompagnamento" mentioned by Mr. Dobson. The "Regole" are simple rules for playing upon a figured bass, as was the custom in the seventeenth and eighteenth centuries. Amid the rules, which are all in Gray's handwriting, are four pieces for the harpsichord, evidently used as studies, in the handwriting of a slap-dash copyist.

VII. The inscription by Gray: "Arie del Sigr. G. B. Pergolese, Napoletano. Firenze, 1740." Five opera airs, three opera duets, and the whole of the famous "Stabat Mater" for two voices and strings are the contents of this volume. The operatic music is from "Catone" and "Olimpiade." The singers mentioned are Farinelli, Monticelli and Viscontina. The last two Gray heard in London in 1742, as is evidenced by the note, "Londra, 1742."

GRAY'S MUSICAL COLLECTION

VIII. A volume of miscellaneous extracts which Gray inscribes as follows: "Arie di Giov. Orlandini, Fiorentino; Franc.co Araia, Dom: Sarri, G: B: Pergolese, Napoletani; Ant: Giaii, Turinese; Giov: Ad.fo·: Hasse, Sassone. Firenze, 1740." The first aria is in the handwriting of Gray, who tells us that Orlandini is "Maestro di Capella al Granduca" (at Florence, obviously). The three airs by this composer are from his opera "Olimpiade," and there is a trio from his "Temistocle." There are three arias by Araia, one air and one duet from Giaii, one air by Sarro from "Achille," as sung by Tesi, nine opera airs by Pergolese and four airs and two duets by Hasse, who fills the place relatively in Gray's collection that he did in the musical life of his period. Several of the airs are dated by the copyist from 1730 to 1735; one he credited to Hasse, and Gray so entered it in his table of contents. Afterward he seems to have learned that the copyist was in error, for he has put his pen through Hasse's name and written above it the name of Pergolese. The singers named are Senesino, Barbieri, Bagnolesi, Tesi, Farinelli, Faustina and Celestina.

IX. Gray's inscription on the cover: "Arie di G. Bta. Lampognani, Andrea

Bernasconi, Milanese; Rinaldo di Capua, Gaetano Latilla, Michele Fini, Napoletani; Gaetano Schiassi, Bolognese; e altri Autori." The "other authors" are disclosed by the table of contents to be Celestino Ligi, Florentine; Carlo Arrigoni, Florentine; Selitti, Neapolitan; Dionigi Zamperelli, Neapolitan; Baldassare Galuppi, Venetian; Riccardo Broschi, Neapolitan, and Mazzoni, Bolognese. There is also an aria by Orlandini, which was overlooked by Gray when he wrote out the table of contents. There are thirty-six numbers in all. One of the airs by Rinaldo di Capua was copied by Gray; over another he has written: "Roma, 1739. Cant: dal Manzuoli." The other singers mentioned are La Turcotti, La Bertolli, La Strada, Farinelli, Amorevoli, Appianino and Babbi.

II

THE POET'S TASTE

THOMAS GRAY was born in 1716 and died in 1771. It is plain enough that he gathered together a large part of his musical collection in 1740, when he was in Italy with his companion Walpole, as Mr. Dobson remarks, though there is evidence in the volumes themselves that all were not compiled at the time. Four of the volumes are dated by Gray 1740, and another can safely be said to have been made at the same time, but the inclusion of some compositions by contemporaries of the poet who had not risen to marked distinction in 1740, like Latilla, Perez and Lampugnani, is an indication that Gray continued to collect music after he had returned to England from Italy. As we shall see presently, his selection is representative of the classic Italian school in opera-writing, and though it is not necessary to an appreciation of his taste to believe that he had heard all the music which he preserved (in fact, it is

A POET'S MUSIC

extremely improbable that he heard some of it), it is nevertheless plain that the collection is an index of his musical predilections and principles. In his biography of the poet the Rev. John Mitford says:

His taste in music was excellent and formed on the study of the great Italian masters who flourished about the time of Pergolesi, as Marcello, Leo and Palestrina; he himself performed upon the harpsichord. And it is said that he sang to his own accompaniment with great taste and feeling.

Gray's knowledge of musical history was plainly better than his biographer's. His careful separation into groups of the composers whose music he collected, as Neapolitans, Florentines, Bolognese and so on, is a proof that he would never have associated Palestrina with men who came upon the scene a whole century after his death. Mason says:

The chief and almost the only one of these (i. e. Gray's) amusements (if we except the frequent experiments he made on flowers in order to mark the mode and progress of their vegetation) was music. His taste in this art was equal to his skill in any more important science. It was founded on the best models, those great masters of Italy

THE POET'S TASTE

who flourished about the same time with his favorite, Pergolese. Of his, of Leo's, Buononcini's, Vinci's and Hasse's works he made a valuable collection while abroad, chiefly of such of their vocal compositions as he had himself heard and admired, observing in his choice of these the same judicious rule which he followed in making his collection of prints, which was not so much to get together complete sets of the works of any master as to select those (the best in their kind) which would recall to his memory the capital pictures, statues and buildings which he had seen and studied. By this means, as he acquired in painting great facility and accuracy in the knowledge of hands, so in music he gained supreme skill in the more refined powers of expression, especially when we consider that art is an adjunct to poetry; for vocal music, and that only (excepting, perhaps, the lessons of the younger Scarlatti), was what he chiefly regarded. His instrument was the harpsichord, on which, though he had little execution, yet when he sung to it he so modulated the small powers of his voice as to be able to convey to the intelligent hearer no common degree of satisfaction. This, however, he could seldom be prevailed upon to do even by his most intimate acquaintances.

In a footnote the writer adds:

He was much admired for his singing in his youth; yet he was so shy in exercising this talent that Mr. Walpole tells me he never could but once prevail on him to give proof of it, and then it was with so much pain to himself that it gave him no manner of pleasure.

Mr. Mason, who wrote thus, was precentor of York Cathedral and knew a thing or two about music. Plainly enough, Mitford had the page which we have just transcribed before him when he wrote his paragraph, though he says that he got the information from Mr. Price. He attempted a little independent flourish when he introduced the name of Palestrina, who, of course, ought to have had the admiration of a man of cultured taste like Gray and probably would have had it had he lived a century and a quarter later than he did, or anticipated the development of an art form not yet called into existence when he died. The flourish resulted like most attempts on the part of the musically illiterate to say something about the art. However, we must be lenient with Mitford. He, too, has his footnote, in which he tells us, as Mr Mason does not, that Gray was not partial to the music of Handel, though Mr. Price had heard him speak with wonder of the chorus in "Jephtha" beginning "No more to Ammon's God and King." Here is confirmation

THE POET'S TASTE

of a suspicion aroused by a piece of negative evidence brought forward by the collection of musical manuscripts. Handel's music is conspicuous by its absence.[1]

In all the nine volumes which we are studying there is not one note of Handel's writing, while there are hundreds of pages of music composed by his rivals. Even Buononcini is mentioned by Mason — the same Buononcini of whom, in the words of the epigram generally ascribed to Swift but in fact the production of John Byrom, some said that, compared with Handel, he was but a "ninny." There is no music of his in the volumes whose contents I have marshalled, but there may be in the volume or volumes of the collection, if such there be, which are missing. In any event, it is strange that, while Mason and the cataloguers of Gray's library mention the names of men who have sunk so deep in the sea of oblivion that we do not know with exactitude when they flourished or what they wrote, they have nothing to say about the giant whose shadow threw all others into eclipse long before the singer of the "Elegy" had

[1] There is the beginning of the air, "Hide me from Day's garish eye" in the volume of fragments which I have mentioned as sold separately in May, 1897.

closed his eyes in death. If Gray collected all his musical manuscripts in Italy, the circumstance affords an explanation which the lovers of Handel can accept as satisfactory. As a composer of operas, Handel's fame may be said to have been confined to London. He began his operatic career in Hamburg, and continued it for a brief space in Italy, but of all the operas which he wrote for London none seems to have been performed on the Continent. In one respect he stood in the estimation of the people who formed the taste of the eighteenth century just where he stands in the estimation of the world to-day. For us the fragments of his operas which remain have only a curious interest; he lives solely in his oratorios and instrumental compositions.

If we assume that Gray's active interest in music began when he was eighteen years old, it is more than likely that he was an active partisan in the contest which brought shipwreck to Handel as an operatic impresario. From 1711, when he opened the Queen's Theatre in the Haymarket (known as "the King's" after the accession of George I), to 1734, Handel had no opposition; but in the latter year, the time which we have set as the beginning of Gray's active participation in musi-

THE POET'S TASTE

cal affairs, the institution known in history as the opera of the "British nobility" was established at the theatre in Lincoln's Inn Fields. Porpora was its director, and his operas were sung; but Porpora's music is also absent from Gray's collection.[1] In the next year the Nobility's opera secured the lease of the King's Theatre, a more serious rebuff than the desertion of Handel's singers to the enemy had been. In two years more both institutions were hopelessly ruined. Handel went back to the King's Theatre, but he was bankrupt in purse, and in 1740, when Gray listened to the operas of his Italian rivals in Florence and Rome, while Horace Walpole "was eating iced fruits in a domino to the sound of a guitar," Handel was producing his last opera, "Deidama." Gray thus appears on the operatic scene as Handel is leaving it, and just in time to see Buononcini (between whom and Handel the author of the epigram already mentioned thought the only difference was that "twixt tweedledum and tweedledee") run away, having been caught pilfering the composition of one of his compatriots. When Handel's rivals get possession of the King's Theatre they bring forward Hasse and his "Artaserse," from which

[1] Except one air in the book of fragments.

opera there are three arias in Gray's collection. They have also Cuzzoni and Senesino, deserters from Handel's company, and a singer new to London in the person of the incomparable Farinelli, who receives many mentions, and Montagnana, who receives none, in Gray's notes. Let us say that the poet hears all that Handel offers during the last three years of the struggle between his institution and that of the *Nobilità Britannica*. There are revivals of old works and six new operas are produced: "Ariodante," "Alcino," "Atalanta," "Arminio," "Giustino" and "Berenice." Carestini sings the principal man's part (in a soprano voice — he was a *musico*) in the first two operas, and Giziello, also a soprano, in the others. Signora Strada, faithful to her master, was the principal woman in all. Memorials to the three exist in the tiny handwriting of Gray on the margins of the poet's books, but they have no reference to Handel's music. Meanwhile the composers of the opposition are Buononcini, Ariosti, Porpora, Vinci, Veracini, Domenico Scarlatti and Galuppi — perhaps, also, Lampugnani and Arrigoni. Of most of these Gray has preserved some music. It is the golden age of the Italian opera, but it is more truthfully reflected to the judgment of to-day in the satirical skits of Addison and Steele than in the eloquent eulogies of its votaries.

Sic transit gloria mundi! Of the composers, specimens of whose skill and style Gray preserved in our nine volumes, scarcely one finds representation on a musical programme of any kind to-day. Search the music shops and you may find a few pieces by Galuppi, whom, also, you may see acclaimed in the pages of a modern poet, who walks upon the ice of musical terminology without a slip; his music you shall not hear though you journey from Dan to Beersheba. They have put a stone in the wall of the house in which he lived in Venice, and some years ago Violet Paget, who knows how to gossip pleasantly about music as well as many other things, attended a festival given in commemoration of the composer. There was much ringing of bells and unfurling of banners and playing of brass bands; but the music was the music of Verdi, Marchetti and their contemporaries. The unheard melodies (which poetical hyperbole would have us believe are sweeter than those heard) in all the festa were Galuppi's. Yet he is but one hundred and twelve years dead, and as I write there lies before me a stained and yellow sheet of ruled paper, inscribed in a handwriting marvellously shaky: "Credo à quarto concerto con stromenti, di Baldassar Galuppi, detto il Buranello, 1780." Poor Galuppi! He was seventy-four years old at the time his trembling fingers penned these notes, and in his day had been the admiration of all Europe. He went to London while Gray was still in Italy — it was in 1741, the year of the quarrel between the poet and Horace Walpole — and stayed over three years. In 1765 Catherine II called him to St. Petersburg, gave him a salary of four thousand rubles, free residence and many other emoluments, and Dr. Burney, who visited him in Venice in 1770, records that "Signor Buranello has preserved all his fire and imagination from the chill blasts of Russia, whence he is lately returned." "This ingenious, entertaining and elegant composer," the learned doctor continues, "abounds in novelty, in spirit and in delicacy," and then he tells of the extraordinary instrumental apparatus used by Galuppi in an overture. There were two orchestras which echoed each other, two organs and "two pair of French horns." Burney, who had been taken to him by Signor Latilla (also on Gray's list) showed him his plans for the great history for which

THE POET'S TASTE

he was gathering material, and was pleased to win the veteran's approval, as also with his definition of good music which, he said, consisted of *vaghezza, chiarezza, e buona modulazione.* — "Beauty, clearness and good modulation." Alas! what would he say to a score of Richard Strauss's?

You shall look in vain in Sir George Grove's musical Pantheon for fully thirteen of the composers whose music Gray thought worth preserving. Orlandini, Giaii, Sarro, Latilla, Fini, Bernasconi, Schiassi, Selitti, Zamperelli, Giacomelli, Broschi, Mazzoni, and Lampugnani, if mentioned in the great "Dictionary of Music and Musicians" at all, are only mentioned incidentally. No information is vouchsafed concerning them, and very little is yielded up to patient research of other sources. Giuseppe Maria Orlandini was a native of Bologna from about 1690, and *Maestro di Capella* to the Grand-duke of Tuscany. No particulars are to be learned of the life of G. A. Giaii, and it is suspected that he is identical with a Signor Gini, who had the same Christian name and was a chapelmaster in Turin in 1728. Gray's copyist mentions Giaii as being "in Turino," and thus gives support to this hypothesis. Domenico Sarro was born in the kingdom of Naples in

1678, and was court chapelmaster about 1706. For the rest, even the names of his operas, all convenient history is silent. Gaetano Latilla was choirmaster of the Conservatorio della Pietà in Venice in 1756, and Galuppi's successor as second chapelmaster at the Church of St. Mark. He is praised for the correctness of his style and his ability as a contrapuntist. Dr. Burney received courtesies at his hands in 1770, and tells us that he was a plain, sensible man about sixty years of age, who had both read and thought much concerning the music of the ancients. In a footnote he adds that he was uncle to Signor Piccini, and author of most of the comic operas " performed in London with such success in the time of Pertici." According to Laborde, Michel Fini was a Neapolitan who wrote a grand opera in 1731–'32 entitled "Gli Sponsali d'Enea," and two intermezzi. Gray preserved an aria from a cantata and numbers from eight operas. Andrea Bernasconi is mentioned by Grove only as the father of that Antonia Bernasconi for whom Gluck wrote "Alceste," and who sang in the "Mitridate" composed by the boy Mozart in 1770–'71 in Milan. He was the son of a French officer, and took up the study of music when he saw his father approaching bankruptcy. His first opera made a hit in Venice in 1741, and in 1755 he became Court chapelmaster in Munich. The singer Bernasconi was his stepdaughter. Gaetano Maria Schiassi was a violinist who composed operas about the period 1732–'35, and also wrote concertos for his instrument. Ligi defeats all our efforts to drag him from obscurity. All that we know we learn from Gray's notes to the effect that he was a Florentine, his Christian name Celestino, and he wrote an opera "Catone." Carlo Arrigoni was also a Florentine, and is supposed to be the "King of Arragon," mentioned among the opponents of Handel in "Harmony in an Uproar."[1] Grove cannot prove his residence in London, but Fétis says that he produced an opera there in 1734. Geminiano Giacomelli was Grand-ducal chapelmaster in Parma, and produced his last opera, "Arsace," in 1736, at Turin. Riccardo Broschi was the brother of Carlo Broschi, called Farinelli, and composed many airs for him. Lampugnani was Galuppi's successor at the opera in London in 1743, and was still active as first harpsichordist, compiler of pasticcios, and singing teacher at Milan when Burney visited that

[1] "Harmony in an Uproar; A Letter to F—d—k H—d—l, Esq." London, 1733.

city in 1770. He is said to have won distinction by his treatment of recitative in his operas.

Impenetrable silence rests upon the rest of Gray's minor list; but something like a lustre shines out from the pages of history which record the achievements of Johann Adolf Hasse, styled "the Saxon," a German, yet the foremost Italian composer of his day, and the husband of the equally famous Faustina Bordoni, who figures in the list of Gray's singers. To her and her colleagues of both sexes in Gray's list I shall presently pay some attention. Just now one of the causes of Hasse's supremacy may be noted. "When the voice was more respected than the servile herd of imitative instruments," says Dr. Burney with a scorn which is fine even if it makes us smile, " and at a time when a different degree and better judged kind of study was perhaps more worthy of attention than at present, the airs of Signor Hasse, particularly those of the pathetic kind, were such as charmed every hearer and fixed the reputation of the first singers in Europe" (such as Farinelli, Faustina, Mingotti, etc.). Concerning Leonardo Leo and Pergolese enough can be learned in the ordinary handbooks, but something must be said touching Rinaldo di

THE POET'S TASTE

Capua and Leonardo Vinci. David Perez was a contemporary of Gray, and the music of his which he preserved Gray copied with his own hand. He was a Spaniard, a chapel-master at Lisbon, and brought out an opera, "Ezio," in London in 1755. He is said to have looked like Handel and, like him, went blind in his old age.

It does not seem altogether right that a man bearing the name of Rinaldo di Capua should be an eighteenth century musician. The flavor of romance goes out from the name. It makes one think of knights in shining steel, of doughty paladins, of joustings and tourneys and of dolorous strokes; also of melodious minstrels, decorous damsels, of hawking and harping and nuptials with great nobley. We hear Rinaldo and think of him who was the Achilles of the Christian army that delivered Jerusalem; we hear Capua and dream of the luxuries which erst threw down the stern manhood of Hannibal. Yet, after all, Rinaldo di Capua was merely a composer, albeit romantically born and a sturdy knight in Apollo's Court. The handbooks know little about him; Sir George Grove's great dictionary nothing at all. Yet his music rang pleasantly in the public ear one hundred and fifty years ago. I open one of the thickest of Gray's manuscript volumes, more than half expecting to see an air from an opera entitled "Gerusalemme Liberata," "Orlando Furioso," "Armida," or even a "Rinaldo" such as Handel composed; alas, the airs which Gray has preserved are taken from a "Demetrio" and a "Vologeso."

It is Dr. Burney who tells us most about Rinaldo di Capua. He visited the composer in Rome when he was making his famous tour of the European continent in search of materials for his great history of music. Rinaldo, he tells us in his "Present State of Music in France and Italy" (a journal of that tour), was the natural son of a person of very high rank in the Neapolitan country. At first he studied music only as an accomplishment, but his father having left him but a small fortune, and it being soon dissipated, he turned to the art as a means of livelihood, composing his first opera at Vienna when he was seventeen years old. Burney forgets to tell us that he was born at Capua, which fact explains his name; being a natural son, he was not permitted to take the name of his father, and had to take that of the city in which he was born, the city whose luxuriousness was the undoing of Hannibal. All of

THE POET'S TASTE

Rinaldo's operas are as dead as he. Mendel's German musical lexicon says that only six of them are known, the score of one of the six, entitled "La Zingara," having been found in Burney's library. Neither of the two works from which Gray quoted is mentioned by Mendel. In Burney's day Rinaldo was accredited with the invention of accompanied recitatives, but this distinction the great historian denied to him after he found specimens of that device in the music of Alessandro Scarlatti. Rinaldo did not himself pretend to the invention. "All that he claims," says Burney, "is the being among the first who introduced long retornellos, or symphonies, into the recitatives of strong passion and distress which express or imitate what it would be ridiculous for the voice to attempt. There are many fine scenes of this kind in his works, and Hasse, Galuppi, Jomelli, Piccini and Sacchini have been very happy in such interesting and often sublime compositions."

Burney, it may be guessed from this last remark, was thoroughly imbued with the musical spirit of his time. He had lived through the period described as that of Gray's early activity, had himself composed dramatic music a few years after Gray came back from Italy, and had heard and praised the new operatic gospel proclaimed by Gluck. But for him there was no absurdity or archaism in the style of composition pursued by his favorite writers. Throughout the eighteenth century the chief dramatic poets of Italy were Apostolo Zeno and Metastasio. The latter in particular was so much admired for the limpidity and beauty of his poetry that his opera books were composed over and over again by the musicians of his time. His "Artaserse" was set no less than forty times, and his "Adriano in Siria" twenty-six. Even Mozart resorted to him for his "Clemenza di Tito." Of the composers represented in Gray's collection, we find that Hasse and Sarro set his "Didone abbandonata," Leo his "Siface," Vinci and Hasse his "Siroë," Vinci his "Catone in Utica," Vinci and Hasse his "Semiramide" (Gluck and Meyerbeer also set this book, but Rossini's libretto is the work of Rossi), Vinci and Hasse his "Alessandro nell' Indie," Vinci, Hasse and Galuppi his "Artaserse" and Hasse alone his "Adriano in Siria," "Ezio," "Olimpiade," "Demofoonte," "La Clemenza di Tito," "Achille in Sciro," "Ciro riconosciuto," "Antigone," "Ipermestra," "Attilio," "Il Rè pastore," "L'Eroe," "Nitetti," "Alcide," "Il

THE POET'S TASTE

Trionfo di Clelia," "Egeria," "Romolo ed Ersilio," "Partenope" and "Il Ruggiero." Indeed, Hasse told Dr. Burney that he had set all of Metastasio's librettos to music except "Temistocle," some of them three or four times over.

Very brave are these names, many of which had done service for Metastasio's predecessors, and right gorgeous was the stage furniture provided for the operas which bore them. But who shall tell the absurdities which characterized the plays themselves and their musical settings? What delicious sport they provided for Addison and Steele! Read the story of the lion which Nicolini slew night after night in "Hydaspes," and the complaint of *Toby Rentfree*, who wanted a reason why he should be treated differently than other subscribers to the opera. Having observed that when gentlemen who were particularly pleased with a song cried out Encore or *Altra volta* the performer was always so obliging as to sing it over, he cried out *Altra volta!* in a very audible voice and with a tolerably good accent, after the combat between Signor Nicolini and the lion; yet so little regard was had for him that the lion was carried off and went to bed without being killed any more that night. An' you would laugh and realize how even in opera there is nothing new under the sun, see, with Addison, Signor Nicolini exposed to a tempest in robes of ermine and sailing in an open boat upon a sea of pasteboard; be entertained with him with painted dragons spitting wildfire (O Wagner!), enchanted chariots drawn by Flanders mares, real cascades in artificial landscapes, and real birds flitting about in painted groves to give verisimilitude to *Almirena's* call upon birds and breezes to tell her of her absent *Rinaldo:*

> *Augelletti che cantate,*
> *Zeffiretti che spirate,*
> *Aure dolce intorno a me,*
> *Il mio ben dite dov' è, etc.*

As the writer once took occasion to say elsewhere,[1] when Senesino, Farinelli, Sassarelli, Ferri and their tribe dominated the stage (and they are the singers who ravished the ears of our gentle poet, who sang a bit himself), it strutted with sexless Agamemnons and Cæsars. Telemachus, Darius, Nero, Cato, Alexander, Scipio and Hannibal ran around on the boards as languishing lovers, clad in humiliating disguises, singing woful arias to their mistress's eyebrows — arias full of trills

[1] "How to Listen to Music," p. 240.

and scales and florid ornaments, but void of feeling as a problem in Euclid. If sentiment was aimed at at all by the composer, it was only a general mood. An air was all gentleness or all fury, and whether gentle or furious, the same flourishes were indulged in when in the course of the air the beloved vowel " A " fell into the proper place in the constructive scheme. *Sangue* or *palpitar*, *stragi* or *amar*, it was all one to the composer and the singer. It was while speaking of the translations of the operas as affected by this style of composition that Addison said :

It often happened, likewise, that the finest notes in the air fell upon the most insignificant words in the sentence. I have known the word " and " pursued through the whole gamut, have been entertained with many a melodious " the," and have heard the most beautiful graces, quavers and divisions bestowed upon " then," " for " and " from "; to the eternal honor of our English particles.

As to the artificiality of the form of the opera, let the reader peruse the following paragraph from Hogarth's " Memoirs of the Opera," remembering that the different kinds of airs referred to were the *Aria Cantabile, Aria di Portamento, Aria di mezzo Carattere,*

A POET'S MUSIC

Aria Parlante (also called *Aria di nota e parola, Aria Agitata, Aria di Strepito,* and *Aria Infuriata*), and *Aria di Bravura* (or *d'agilita*):

In the structure of an opera the number of characters was generally limited to six, three of each sex; and, if it was not a positive rule, it was at least a practice hardly ever departed from, to make them all lovers; — a practice, the too slavish adherence to which introduced feebleness and absurdity into some of the finest works of Metastasio. The principal male and female singers were, each of them, to have airs of all the different kinds. The piece was to be divided into three acts, and not to exceed a certain number of verses. It was required that each scene should terminate with an air; that the same character should not have two airs in succession; that an air should not be followed by another of the same class; and that the principal airs of the piece should conclude the first and second acts. In the second and third acts there should be a scena consisting of an accompanied recitative, an air of execution, and a grand duet sung by the hero and heroine. There were occasional choruses; but trios and other concerted pieces were unknown except in the opera buffa, where they were beginning to be introduced.

There's your recipe for the concoction of an eighteenth century Italian opera. Small

THE POET'S TASTE

wonder that industrious composers could turn them out by the dozen — smaller wonder that it finally dawned on some of the composers themselves that they were getting to be very monotonous in their music. And here we must shout a bravo for our Capuan Rinaldo, who told Dr. Burney, to the evident pain of that distinguished traveller, that there was nothing left for the composers of his time to do but to write themselves and others over again, and that the only chance which they had left for obtaining the reputation of novelty and invention arose either from ignorance or want of memory in the public, as everything, both in melody and modulation, worth doing had often already been done. He did not except himself from his censure, but confessed that though he had written full as much as his neighbors, "yet out of all his works, perhaps not above one new melody can be found, which has been wire-drawn in different keys and different measures a thousand times." Bravo Rinaldo! *Altra volta!*

Over two hundred and twenty-five years lie between the times of Leonardo da Vinci, the painter, and Leonardo Vinci, the composer; yet they have been confounded even by writers on music. The painter, like *Sir*

A POET'S MUSIC

Andrew Aguecheek, could play on the "viol de gamboys," but he was not an opera composer; probably because the opera was not invented until seventy-five years after his death, whereas his namesake, the musician, was one of the chief glories of the operatic stage in the first half of the eighteenth century. He had been dead about ten years when Gray visited Italy, but the excellent repute in which his music was held is attested by the preservation of the cantata which he composed in 1729 for the birthday of the French dauphin. He was a royal chapel-master, and member of a monkish order, and yet a gay man of the world. This was his undoing. He died of poison, administered to him in chocolate, it is said, by a certain noble lady, concerning whose relations with himself he spoke boastfully in public once too often. I have already mentioned the originality shown in the instrumental part of the birthday cantata "La Contesa di Numi." Burney says his operas form an era in dramatic music, by the direct simplicity and emotion which he threw into the natural, clear and dramatic strains of his airs and by the expressive character of the accompaniments, especially those of the obbligato recitatives. "Virgil himself," said Count Algarotti, speak-

THE POET'S TASTE

ing of Vinci's "Didone Abbandonata," "would have been pleased to hear a composition so animated and so terrible, in which the heart and soul were at once assailed by all the powers of music."

III

LAST CENTURY SINGERS

ARRANGED in alphabetical order, the list of singers whose names are recorded in the nine manuscript volumes of music collected by Gray is as follows: Appianino, Amorevoli, Babbi, Bagnolesi, Barbieri, Bertolli, Carestini, Celestina, Cuzzoni, Farfallino, Farinelli, Faustina, Gizziello, Lorenzino, Manzuoli, Monticelli, Scalzi, Senesino, Strada, Tesi, Turcotti and Viscontina. Many of these singers are as completely lost to the world as the composers who wrote for them, but in the list there are half a dozen names which stand in letters of gold in the history of *bel canto*. Farinelli, we have been led to believe, was the greatest singer that ever lived, and one of the things which Gray's music can teach us is that, taking the art for what it was one hundred and fifty years ago, the greatest operatic artists of to-day are the merest tyros compared with him. It would be idle to attempt comparisons on any other basis than mere technical skill, however. In the arrangement of the names in the list no regard was had to the consideration of sex, and it might furnish amusement for an idle moment if the reader were to attempt to separate the men from the women. It would be a fair wager to lay big odds against one student of musical history in a hundred succeeding in making the division correctly. The men and women, as a matter of fact, are about evenly divided, but if sex of voice were to be the determining factor, instead of physical sex, a very different result would be reached. Though half of the singers were men and half women, nine-tenths of the voices were sopranos and contraltos. The normal voices of men were not in favor in the days of the gentle Gray. There were tenor and bass parts in the operas of Hasse and contemporary composers, but they belonged to subordinate characters in the play, and the singers to whom they fell were not considered of particular consequence. It was the day of artificiality in music as well as manners. Handel, whose taste was cast in a manlier mould than that of his rivals, showed notable respect for the bass voice in parts written for singers named Roschi, Reimschneider, Reinhold and Waltz, whose names are identified with bass songs published at the time. In all probability all four were Germans. The

A POET'S MUSIC

last three certainly were, and the name of the first sounds like a transmogrification from the German. Reimschneider came from Hamburg, and was thus announced by Handel in the advertisement of his company in 1829: "A bass voice from Hamburgh; there being none worth engaging in Italy." Yet basses were more practicable than tenors, who had no occupation at a time when operatic lovers were all sopranos or contraltos. The musico yielded his place to the tenor before the eighteenth century expired, though he still had representatives on the stage in the earliest decades of the nineteenth; and now, a hundred years later, there are indications that the monopoly of the tenor is at an end, and that the next generation will accept a bass or barytone lover as we accept the tenor to-day and Gray accepted the musico.

It is the male soprano or contralto who fills the greater part of the book of song in the golden age of the Italian opera. Porpora, Bernacchi and Pistocchi were the lawgivers in the vocal art, and the pupils who brought them fame were musicos. There were famous women, too, and though they managed to excite social wars, like that which divided London into two camps in the operatic consulate of Handel, they were never

LAST CENTURY SINGERS

quite the popular idols that Farinelli, Senesino and their tribe became. Of Gray's women singers four deserve to be called great — Faustina, Cuzzoni, Tesi and Strada. The rivalry between the first two led to one of the most famous warfares on record. Cuzzoni was the first on the field in London, whither she came in 1723, engaged by Handel. She had a wonderfully sweet voice, and though not pretty of features or figure she enchanted the subscribers to the opera. Already at her second performance the directors, who had engaged to pay her two thousand guineas for the season (the story was told that she refused the equivalent of forty-eight thousand guineas for a season in Italy), raised the price of tickets to four guineas. But the salary question was made to be her undoing. A few years later, at the very heyday of her popularity and height of her rivalry with Faustina, some of her supporters in the nobility persuaded her to make a vow that she would not take a penny less salary than Faustina received. She had worn out her popularity with the directors by this time, and they took advantage of her vow to rid themselves of her. When it came to a renewal of contracts they offered Faustina one guinea more than Cuzzoni, and the latter left

A POET'S MUSIC

London. Had Cuzzoni's amiability been as great as her musical gifts she would probably have held out against the rivalry of Faustina better than she did. At first she had the town completely with her. For a whole year immediately before the arrival of Faustina in 1726 her costume in "Rodelinda" set the fashion for the ladies of London, who wore brown silk gowns, embroidered with silver. But she was capricious and ill-tempered. It was the devil in Cuzzoni that Handel threatened to cast out in the name of Beelzebub, the prince of devils, when he dragged her to an open window and threatened to hurl her out on the stone pavement below unless she sang one of his airs as he had written it. She came back to London in 1749, but never regained her old popularity, and her last days were pitiful in the extreme. She disappeared from public view, and is said to have supported herself in her old age in Bologna by working at the trade of button-making.

Faustina had a nature which was as lovely as Cuzzoni's voice, and a voice which in a sense offered a parallel to Cuzzoni's nature. She was a noble Venetian, beautiful of features and form, with a mezzo-soprano voice reaching from B-flat below (one air in the Gray books goes down to A natural) to G *in alt*, but which was rather hard and brilliant. She had a "fluent tongue," 't is said, but was wise enough to use its fluency in singing rather than in gossip or controversy with opera directors. In her warfare with Cuzzoni she had the men on her side and Cuzzoni the women. The most notable illustration of this division of sentiment was to be seen in the household of Sir Robert Walpole, when the noble lord fought under the banner of Faustina and his lady wore the colors of Cuzzoni. But the lady was the better diplomat of the two, and used to have both singers as her guests at the same time without disturbance of the peace, though eventually they did fall to it tooth and nail in the face of the public. The Countess of Pembroke led the Cuzzoni faction, which seems to have been the first to resort to such disgraceful methods as hissing on the entrance of the rival singer. Wherefore we have preserved for us an epigram to this effect:

> Old poets sing that beasts did dance
>   Whenever Orpheus play'd;
> So, to Faustina's charming voice,
>   Wise Pembroke's asses bray'd.

Faustina married the composer Hasse, who was ten years her junior; but he was the most popular composer of his time and director of the opera in Dresden — one of the leading establishments of Europe. She got a fifteen years' engagement at the Saxon capital, and then retired. Dr. Burney visited her when she was seventy-two years old and asked her to sing. *Ah, non posso!* she replied; *ho perduto tutte le mie facoltà.* ("Alas, I cannot. I have lost all my faculties.")

The contralto voice was held in higher honor in the eighteenth century than now, probably because it was as often found in the throats of unsexed men as the soprano. The greatest of the contralto singers, moreover, was more of a man than Farinelli, notwithstanding that he came near being Prime Minister of Spain. Vittoria Tesi-Tramontini had a contralto voice so strong, so deep and so masculine in quality that in 1719, when she was engaged at Dresden, she used to sing bass airs *all' ottava*. Yet she was so much of a woman that it is suspected that she is the young artist who fell so violently in love with Handel in 1707 that she followed him from theatre to theatre in Italy in order to sing in his operas. At eighty-odd years of age the Tesi was still alive and a resident of Vienna where Dr. Burney visited her. "The great singer Signora Tesi, who was a celebrated performer, upwards of fifty years ago, lives here," writes the Doctor in his "Present State":

She is now more than eighty but has long quitted the stage. She has been very sprightly in her day, and yet is at present in high favour with the Empress-queen. Her story is somewhat singular. She was connected with a certain count, a man of great quality and distinction, whose fondness increased by possession to such a degree as to determine him to marry her: a much more uncommon resolution in a person of high birth on the continent than in England. She tried to dissuade him; enumerated all the bad consequences of such an alliance; but he would listen to no reasoning, nor take any denial. Finding all remonstrances vain, she left him one morning, went into a neighbouring street and addressing herself to a poor labouring man, a journeyman baker, said she would give him fifty ducats if he would marry her, not with a view of their cohabiting together but to serve a present purpose. The poor man readily consented to become her nominal husband; accordingly they were married; and when the count renewed his solicitations she told him it was now utterly impossible to grant his request, for she was already the wife of another; a sacrifice she had made to his fame and family.

A POET'S MUSIC

Of the men singers in Gray's list the names that live freshest in musical history are Farinelli, Senesino and Caffarelli. A few of the others are known to special students, but the

A CADENZA BY HASSE, SUNG BY TESI.

memory of the rest has disappeared with the tribe to which they belonged. Of Appianino nothing has been found, in spite of diligent research. There are faint traces of Babbis in the record of singers, one of whom was a tenor in the second half of the eighteenth century, but he cannot be the singer named by Gray, for the copyist wrote the name on the sheet in 1740 or earlier. Giovanni Manzuoli did not sing in London until 1764, only seven years before Gray died, but the poet heard him in Rome in 1739. He was a soprano, born in 1725, of whom Farinelli thought well enough to engage him for Madrid in 1753. When the boy Mozart was in Italy in 1770 and 1771 a warm friendship sprung up between Manzuoli and the young genius and his father. He sang in a serenata composed by Mozart (then fifteen years old) in honor of the nuptials of Archduke Ferdinand, at Milan in 1771, and in one of his letters sent to the family at Salzburg Papa Mozart tells how a few weeks later he was engaged at the opera for five hundred ducats. No mention of an honorarium for the serenata having been made in the decree of appointment, Manzuoli demanded five hundred ducats more. The court sent him seven hundred ducats and a gold box, but the singer indignantly returned both and left the city. Angelo Amorevoli was in London during the season of 1741, but most of his career was spent as a member of the opera at Dresden, where he died in 1798. Lorenzino has eluded all research; so has Farfallino; but as the custom, which still prevails, of Italianizing the names of singers was very common in the eighteenth century, the former may have been a German singer named Lorenz. Carlo Scalzi came to London, where he had sung previously, to join Handel's forces in 1733. He returned with Durastanti, who had been forced off the field by Cuzzoni in 1724. Gioacchino Conti, called Gizziello, was a sopranist, and in the front ranks of his kind. He was born in 1714, and sang in London for Handel in 1736. Burney says he was so modest that when he first heard Farinelli at a rehearsal he burst into tears and fainted away with despondency. One of the prettiest stories of the enthusiasm which his singing created couples his name with Caffarelli's. This great singer, being engaged at Naples, travelled all night to hear the young man at Rome who was threatening to become a dangerous rival. He went into the pit of the theatre, muffled in a cloak, so that his presence might not be known, but after

Gizziello's first air he arose and shouted: *Bravo! bravissimo Gizziello! E Caffarelli che ti lo dice!* ("'Tis Caffarelli who says so.") Carestini was a member of Handel's company for seven years, from 1733, when he took the place of Senesino, who had gone to the company of the nobility. At the beginning of his career his voice was a strong and clear soprano, but it afterward changed into the fullest, finest and deepest counter tenor that had ever been heard in London. He sang in Berlin from 1750 to 1755, and died soon after he retired to Italy, having maintained a reputation of the highest order on the stage for more than thirty years. Angelo Maria Monticelli was in London from 1741 to 1746. Gray notes an air from Pergolese's "Alessandro" as sung by him in London in 1742.

The books are full of stories about the great triumvirate, Farinelli, Senesino and Caffarelli. The last sang in London in 1738, after the departure of Farinelli, and, though there were judges who thought him the equal of that wonderful man, he was not successful with the English. Caffarelli grew wealthy enough to buy an Italian dukedom for his nephew, and reared for himself a magnificent palace, on the doors of which he put the modest inscription:

A POET'S MUSIC

> AMPHION THEBAS, EGO DOMUM.

All readers of musical history know that at the height of his popularity Farinelli was called to Madrid by the Queen of Spain to

Fugge il mi-o sa — ngue al cuor.

A CADENZA BY HASSE, SUNG BY
FARINELLI.

cure Philip V of the dulness which had settled over his spirits. It is the story of King Saul and David over again. Philip loved music, and Farinelli won so great an influence over him the first time that he sang that he persuaded the king to be shaved, look after his raiment and attend to affairs of state. A salary of three thousand pounds sterling was settled upon him, and he became so powerful at court that he was looked upon as Philip's prime minister. Every night for ten years Farinelli sang for the king in his chamber, and sang the same four songs. One of these songs is in the Gray collection. It is an *aria cantabile* from Hasse's "Artaserse":

> *Per questo dolce amplesso,*
> *Per questo estremo addio*
> *Serbami, o padre mio,*
>   *L' idolo amato,*

the melody of which begins as follows:

A POET'S MUSIC

One of the incidents of Senesino's London career is told in Lady Mary Wortley Montagu's sparkling letters. The musico was indiscreet enough to fall in love with the singer Anastasia Robinson, who became Lady Peterborough, and make protestation of his passion. She reported the fact to Lord Peterborough, who caned Senesino behind the scenes till he fell on his knees and begged for mercy. "Poor Senesino," says Lady Mary, "like a vanquished knight, was forced to confess upon his knees that Anastasia was a nonpareil of virtue and beauty. Lord Stanhope (afterward Lord Chesterfield), as dwarf to the said giant, joked on his side and was challenged for his pains."

HAYDN IN LONDON

I

HIS NOTE BOOK

IT is known to all readers of the biographies of Haydn that he twice visited London. On his first visit he spent all of the year 1791 and a portion of 1792 in the English capital. His second visit was made in 1794 and 1795. The incidents of these visits have been related in detail by C. F. Pohl in his book "Mozart and Haydn in London," published in 1867, an invaluable help for all who wish to study the music and musicians of London at the close of the last century. In the preparation of this book Pohl made use of a diary kept by Haydn on his first visit, the original of which came into the possession of Joseph Weigl, a well-known musician, who was not only the friend but also the godson of Haydn. A similar record of the second visit was kept by Haydn, but this was lost, and Weigl's treasure was only saved from destruction by the carefulness of a kitchenmaid who made a final inquiry as to whether the two little books were of further use as she was about to consign them to the fire. The precious autograph afterward came into the possession of Pohl, and is doubtless safely housed in some German library, though of that I cannot speak definitely.

A copy which the late Alexander W. Thayer, Beethoven's biographer, had made in 1862 is now in my possession. The notes are contained in two small books interleaved with blotting paper and the copyist seems to have reproduced the style and form of the original autograph in every particular. Many of the entries are not dated and chronological order is not preserved, so that it would, perhaps, be more correct to call the books memorandum books instead of a diary, Haydn's purpose seemingly having been to use them in later years to refresh his memory. Some entries are merely vague, mnemonic hints and one which descants in epigrammatic manner on the comparative morals of the women of France, Holland and England, is unfit for publication. I transcribe, translate and publish the entries not as thinking that they will add to the world's knowledge of last century music, but because the utterances will help to an appreciation of the personal character of the composer of "The Creation."

HIS NOTE BOOK

Needle, scissors and a little knife for Mrs. v. Kees.

For Biswanger, spectacles for from 50 to 60 years.

For Hamburger, scissors to cut finger nails and a larger pair.

A woman's watch chain.

For Mrs. Genzinger, various things.

Plainly a memorandum of purchases to be made for home friends.

Head of Juno, white Cornelian 6 guinees.
that other white red Cornelian 3½ guinees.
6 Schiots (?)   8   "
12 deto   12   "
Watch from gold   30   "
the Chen   1   "

This memorandum being in English I reproduce it *verb. et lit.*

On November 5th I was a guest at the dinner of the Lord Mayor. At the first table sat the new Lord Mayor with his wife, then the Lord Canceler (Chancellor) the two Scherifs (sheriffs) Duc de Lids (Duke of Leeds) Minister Pitt and the other judges of the first class. At No. 2 I ate with Mr. Silvester, the greatest lawyer and first Alderman of London. There were sixteen tables in this room (which is called Geld [Guild] Hall) besides others in adjoining rooms; in all nearly 1200 persons dined, all with great pomp. The viands were neat and well-cooked; wine of many kinds and in superfluity. The company sat down at 6 o'clock and arose at 8. The Lord Mayor was escorted according to rank and with many ceremonies before and after dinner; his sword and a sort of gold crown were carried before him and there was music of trumpets and a brass band. After dinner the distinguished company of table No. 1 retired to a separate room to drink coffee and tea; we other guests were taken into another room. At 9 o'clock No. 1 goes into a smaller hall whereupon the ball begins; in this hall there is, *à parte*, an elevated place for the high *nobless* where the Lord Mayor is seated upon a sort of throne with his wife. The dancing then begins according to rank, but only a couple at a time as at court on the King's birthday, January 6th (June 4). In this small hall there are raised benches where for the greater part the fair sex reigns. Nothing but minuets are danced in this room; but I could n't stay longer than a quarter of an hour; first, because of the heat caused by so many people being crowded into so small a room, second, because of the wretched dance music, two violins and one violoncello composing the whole orchestra. The minuets were more Polish than German or Italian. Thence I went into another room which looked more like a subterranean cave. There the dance was English; the music was a little better because there was a drum which drowned the blunders of the fiddlers. I went on to the great hall where we had dined; the music was more sufferable. The dance was English but only on the elevated platform where the Lord Mayor and the first four members had dined. The other tables were all newly surrounded by men who, as usual, drank right lustily all night long. The most singular thing of all, however, was the fact that a part of the company danced on without hearing a note of the music, for first at one table, then at another, some were howling songs and some drinking toasts amidst the maddest shrieks of " Hurra! Hurra!" and the swinging of glasses. The hall and all the other rooms are illuminated with lamps which give out an unpleasant odor, particularly in the small dance hall. It is remarkable that the Lord Mayor needs no knife at table, as a carver, who stands in front of him in the middle of the table, cuts up everything for him.

Behind the Lord Mayor there is another man who shouts out all the toasts with might and main; after each shout follow trumpets and drums. No toast was more applauded than that to the health of Mr. Pitt. Otherwise, however, there is no order. This dinner cost one thousand six hundred pounds; one half is paid by the Lord Mayor, the other half by the two sheriffs. A Lord Mayor is newly elected every year; he wears over his cos-

HAYDN IN LONDON

tume a wide black satin mantle, in shape like a domino, richly ornamented in bands of gold lace especially about the arms. Around his neck is a massive gold chain like that of our order of the *Toison;* his wife also wears one and she is My-lady, and remains such ever after. The entire ceremony is noteworthy, particularly the procession on the Tems (Thames) from the Guildhall to West-Mynster.

Mistress Schroeter, No. 6 James-st. Buckinghamgate.

Thereby hangs a tale which I reserve for a separate chapter.

The national debt of England is estimated to be over two hundred millions. Once it was calculated that if it were desired to pay the debt in silver, the wagons that would bring it, close together, would reach from London to York (two hundred miles), each wagon carrying £6,000.

Mr. Hunter is the greatest and most celebrated Chyrurgus in London. Leicester Square.

Dr. Hunter became Haydn's friend, and tried hard to persuade the composer to permit him to remove a polypus from his nose; but in vain.

HIS NOTE BOOK

N. B. Mr. Silvester, Chamberlain of the Duchess of York.

Que l'amitié soit aussi solide. N. B. Lady Blake from Langham.

On June 3ᵈ 1792 I dined with M. and Madame Mara, Mr. Kely (Michael Kelly), & Madame Storace at the house of her brother Storace. *Sapienti pauca.*

On May 30ᵗʰ, 1792, the great Widows' concert, which last year was given for the last time in Westminster Abbey with 885 persons, took place in St. Margaret's Church because of the too great expense. There were 800 persons at the rehearsal and 2000 at the concert.

The King gives 100 guineas each time.

Pohl gives us the details of this concert as he does of nearly all the concerts or other public functions which Hadyn attended. He puts the date a day later than Haydn, however, and calls the concert, more correctly, the annual benefit of the Royal Society of Musicians. At the command of the King the orchestra and chorus of the Concerts of Ancient Music participated without remuneration. Dr. Arnold conducted, Cramer was leader, Dr. Dupuis played the organ, and the principal singers were Madame Mara, Mr.

HAYDN IN LONDON

Kelly and Bartleman. As was the custom "The Messiah" was performed and at the command of the King, given by a gesture, "For unto us a child is born," "Hallelujah," and "Worthy is the Lamb" were repeated.

The trial of Hastings (Warren Hastings) last week, May 25, 1792, was the ninety-second meeting in Westminster Hall. Hasting (sic) has individually three advocates. Each of these gets ten guineas on the day of meeting. The case had its beginning four years ago. It is said that Hastings is worth a million pounds sterling.

On June 15 I went from Windsor to Slough to Dr. Herschel, where I saw the great telescope. It is 40 feet long and 5 feet in diameter. The machinery is vast, but so ingenious that a single man can put it in motion with ease. There are also two smaller telescopes, of which one is 22 feet long and magnifies six thousand times. The King had two made for himself, of which each measures 12 *Schuh*. He gave him one thousand guineas for them. In his younger days Dr. Herschel was in the Prussian service as an oboe player. In the seven-years' war he deserted with his brother and came to England. For many years he supported himself with music, became organist at Bath, turned, however, to astronomy. After providing himself with the necessary instruments he left Bath, rented a room not far from Windsor, and studied day and night. His landlady was a widow. She fell in love with him, married him, and gave him a dowry of 100,000 £. Besides this he has 500 £ for life, and his wife, who is forty-five years old, presented him with a son this year, 1792. Ten years ago he had his sister come; she is of the greatest service to him in his observations. Frequently he sits from five to six hours under the open sky in the severest cold.

To-day, January 14, 1792, the life of Madam Bilingthon (Billington) was published in print. It is a shameless exposure. The publisher is said to have gotten possession of her letters and to have offered to give them back to her for 10 guineas; otherwise he would print them. She, however, did not want to spend the 10 guineas, and, demanded the letters through the courts. Her application was rejected, and she took an appeal, but in vain. Her opponent, nevertheless, offered her 500 £. The book appeared to-day, but there was not another copy to be had till 3 o'clock. It is said that her character is very faulty, but, nevertheless, she is a great genius, and all the women hate her because she is so beautiful. N. B. — She is said to have written all these shameful letters, which contain accounts of her amours, to her mother. She is said to be an illegitimate child, and it is now believed that her reputed father is concerned in the affair. Such stories are common in London; the husband provides opportunities for his wife in order to profit by it and relieve his victim of £1,000 or more.

The scandalous book referred to was the "Memoirs of Mrs. Billington. Printed for James Ridgway, London, York street, St. James's Sq., 1792." It would be quite as idle to justify this book as to defend the notorious character of Mrs. Billington. It is a sufficient commentary on the times that such a book could appear and such a career as that of Mrs. Billington be led without invoking effective popular condemnation; but it must be remembered that Mrs. Billington was far and away the greatest singer of native birth (her parents were German) who had been heard and that she was as much admired for her artistic skill as for her physical beauty. Michael Kelly wrote of her in his Memoirs: "I thought her an angel in beauty and the Saint Cecilia of song." Sir Joshua Reynolds painted a portrait of her in the character of Saint Cecilia, a fact which gave Signor Carpani one of the prettiest anecdotes in his "Le Haydine," a book that the scoundrel Beyle,

HIS NOTE BOOK

known in catalogues as Bombet, shamelessly plagiarized in his " Lettres écrites de Vienne sur le célebre J. Haydn." Here it is:

He often saw, in London, the celebrated Mrs. Billington, whom he enthusiastically admired. He found her one day sitting to Reynolds, the only English painter who has succeeded in portraits. He had just taken that of Mrs. Billington in the character of St. Cecilia listening to the celestial music, as she is usually drawn. Mrs. Billington showed the picture to Haydn. "It is like," said he, "but there is a strange mistake." "What is that?" asked Reynolds, hastily. "You have painted her listening to the angels; you ought to have represented the angels listening to her." Mrs. Billington sprung up, and threw her arms around his neck. It was for her that he composed his "Ariadne abbandonata," which rivals that of Benda.

A neat story. Pity that Pohl tries to spoil it by pointing out that Sir Joshua painted Mrs. Billington's portrait in 1790, a year before Haydn came to London. The painting was bought at auction by an American in 1845 for five hundred and five guineas.

On the 14th of June I went to Windsor and thence 8 miles to Ascot Heath to see the races. The races are run on a large field, especially prepared for them, in which there is a circular (track) 2 English miles long and 6 fathoms (*Klafter*) wide all very smooth and even. The whole field has a gentle ascent. At the summit the circle becomes a straight line of 2 thousand paces, and on this line there are booths, amphitheatres, of various sizes capable of holding 2 to 3 hundred persons. The others are smaller. In the middle is one for the Prince Wallis (sic) and other dignitaries. The places in the booths cost from 1 to 42 shillings per person. Opposite the booth of the Prince Wallis there is a high stage, with a bell over it, and on the stage stand a number of appointed and elected sworn persons who give the first signal with the bell for the performers to range up in front of the stage. When all is ready the bell is rung a second time and at the first stroke they ride off and whoever returns first to the stage after traversing the circle of two miles receives the prize. In the first Heath (heat) there were three riders who were compelled to go around the circle twice without stopping. They did it in 5 minutes. No stranger will believe it unless he is convinced. The second time there were seven and when they reached the middle of the circle the seven were in line, but when they approached some fell back, but never more than about 10 paces and when one thinks that one rider, who is about to reach the goal, will be the first in which moment large wagers are laid on him, another rushes past him with inconceivable *Force* and reaches the winning place. The rider is very lightly clad in silk, each of a different color, so as to make it easier to recognize them, without boots a little *cascet* (sic) on his head, all lean as a greyhound and their horses. Each is weighed and a certain weight is allowed him adjusted *a proportione*, and if the rider is too light he must put on heavier clothes, or lead is hung on him. The horses are of the finest breeds, light, with very thin feet, the hair of the neck tied into braids, the hoofs very neat. As soon as they hear the sound of the bell they dash off with the greatest *Force*. Every leap of the horses is 22 feet long. These horses are very dear. Prince Wallis a few years ago paid 8 thousand pounds for one and sold it again for 6 thousand pounds. But the first time he won with it 50,000 pounds. Amongst others a single large booth has been erected where the Englishmen make their bets. The King has his own booth at one side. I saw 8 Heats the first day, and in spite of a heavy rain 2000 vehicles, all full of people and 3 times as many people were present on foot. Besides this there are all kinds of puppet-plays Ciarlatanz (sic) and conjurors and buffoons, during the races and in a multitude of tents food, all kinds of wine and beer. Also a large number of Io-players (in English it is written Eo) which game is prohibited in London. The races take place five days in succession. I was present on the second day. The sport began at 2 o'clock and lasted till 5, the third day till half-past six though there were but 3 Heaths (sic) for the reason that twice three ran and each winning once a fourth trial had to be made to decide.

If anybody steals £2 he is hanged; but if I trust anybody with £2000 and he carries it off with him to the devil, he is acquitted.

Murder and forgery can not be pardoned. Last year a Pope (clergyman) was hanged for the latter notwithstanding the King himself did all he could for him.

The city of London consumes annually 800,000 cartloads of coal. Each cart holds thirteen bags, each bag two *Metzen*. Most of the coal comes from Newcastle. Often 200 vessels laden with coal arrive at the same time. A cartload costs 2½£. In 1795 (?) the price of a cartload was 7£.

Thirty-eight thousand houses have been built within the last thirty years.

If a woman murders her husband she is burned alive; a husband, on the contrary, is hanged.

The punishment of a murderer is aggravated by ordering his "anatomization" in the death sentence.

On January 14, 1792, the Pantheon Theatre burned down two hours after midnight.

HIS NOTE BOOK

On May 21 Giardini's concert took place in Renalag (Ranelagh Gardens). He played like a pig.

Giardini was a popular violinist. Haydn, always amiable, tried to meet him in a friendly spirit, but Giardini said: "I don't want to see the German dog." Evidently Haydn got even with him in this note.

On June 12th I attended Mara's *benefice* in the great Haymarket Theatre. "Dido" with music by Sarti was played. N. B. Only a terzetto, a few recitatives and a little aria were composed by Sarti. The other pieces were by 6 other and different masters. The *1ma Dona* sang an old aria by Sacchini: *Son Regina* etc.

An Archbishop of London, having asked Parliament to silence a preacher of the Moravian religion who preached in public, the Vice-President answered that could easily be done; only make him a Bishop, and he would keep silent all his life.

In Oxford-Street I saw a copper-plate of St. Peter clad as a priest with outstretched arms. On the right hand shines the glory of heaven; on the left you see the devil whispering in his ear, and on his head he wore a wind-mill.

On the 1st of June, 1792 was Mara's *benefice*.

HAYDN IN LONDON

Two of my symphonies were played and I accompanied on the pianoforte alone a very *difficult* English aria by Purcell. The *Compagnie* was very small.

In the month of June, 1792, a chicken 7 shillings, an *Indian* 9 shillings, a dozen larks 1 *Coron*. N. B. If plucked a duck 5 shillings.

On the 3^d of June, being the eve of the King's birthday, all the bells in London are rung from 8 o'clock in the morning till 9, and so also in honor of the Queen.

February 8th 1792 the first Ancient Concert took place.

On the 13th of February the Professional Concerts began.

The 17th Salomon's Concert.

ANECTOD. (sic) At a grand concert as the director was about to begin the first number the kettledrummer called loudly to him, asking him to wait a moment, because his two drums were not in tune. The leader could not and would not wait any longer, and told the drummer to transpose for the present.

While Mr. Fox was seeking votes to elect him to Parliament a citizen told him that instead of

HIS NOTE BOOK

a vote he would give him a rope. Fox replied that he would not rob him of an heirloom.

Duchess of Devonchire (Devonshire), his protector. Anecdote about the foot under her petticoat.

N. B. from *Würmland:*
Quoties cum stercore certo vico vel vincor semper ego maculor.
Ex nihilo nihil fit.
Domine, praxis est multiplex, qui n' intelligit est simplex.
Stella a stella differt claritate, non eadem lux omnibus.
Lord, all is not light that lightens!
Interesse toto mundo
Sin fronte colitur
Sine satis, sine fundo
Interque quaeritur.

Mel in core, verba lactis
Fel in corde, fraus in factis.
Superernumerarius — the fifth wheel of a wagon.
Mens, ratio, et consilium in senibus est.
Si nisi non esset, perfectus quilibet esset raro sunt visi qui caruêre nisi.

Eight days before Pentecost I heard 4,000 charity children sing the following song in St. Paul's Church. One performer beat time to it.

HAYDN IN LONDON

No music has ever moved me so much in my life as this devotional and innocent piece:

N. B. — All the children are newly clad, and walk in in procession. The organist played the melody neatly and simply, and then all began to sing at once.

Haydn's experience at this meeting of the charity children has been the subject of much comment in England. His sensations at hearing the music of the children and other choristers were duplicated half a century later in Berlioz, who wrote a description of the meeting of 1851 for the "Journal des Debats," and told how he put on a surplice, took a place among the bass singers, and was so moved by the stupendous sonority of the choir that, "like Agamemnon with his toga," he hid his face behind his music-book. Duprez, the tenor, who was also present, grew terribly excited. Berlioz says: "I never saw Duprez in such a state. He stammered, wept and raved." J. B. Cramer was also present, and, rushing up to Berlioz as he was leaving the cathedral, shouted: *Cosa stupenda! Stupenda! La gloria dell' Inghilterra.* ("Stupendous! Stupendous! The glory of England!") At the meeting which Haydn attended the children also sang the "Old Hundredth" Psalm. The hymn of which he notes the melody is Jones's Chant. John Jones was organist of St. Paul's at the time. The chant has since been supplanted. It is singular that Haydn wrote down the melody in the key of E, though it was sung in D.

In the year 1791 22 thousand persons died in London.

Lokhart (Lockhart) blind organist.

> *Io vi mando questo foglio*
> *Dalle lagrime rigato,*
> *Sotto scritto dal cordoglio*
> *Dai pensieri sigillato*
> *Testimento del mio amore*
> *(Io) vi mando questo core.*

HAYDN IN LONDON

February 13th 1792, the first Professional Concert took place.

On the 17th Salomon's Concert.

On the evening of March 20th, 1792, there was a thunderstorm. An unusual thing in London.

An apprentice generally works all the year round from 6 o'clock in the morning till 6 in the evening, and in this time has not more than an hour and a half at his own disposition. He gets a guinea a week, but must find himself. Many are paid by the piece, but every quarter of an hour of absence is docked. Blacksmiths' apprentices are obliged to work an hour a day longer.

To-day, June 4, 1792, I was in Vauxhall where the birthday of the King was celebrated. Over 30,000 lamps were burning, but very few people were present, owing to the cold. The place and its diversions have no equal in the world. There are 155 dining booths scattered about, all very neat, and each comfortably seating six persons. There are very large alleys of trees, the branches meeting overhead in a splendid roof of foliage. Coffee and milk cost nothing. You pay half a crown for admission. The music is fairly good. A stone statue of Handel is to be seen. On the 2^d inst. there was a masked ball; the management made 3,000 guineas in a single night.

HIS NOTE BOOK

Singers in London.		Compositores.
Mara	Bacchierotti	Baumgarten
Storace	Kelly	Clementi
Billingthon	Davide	Dussok. Dussek
Cassentini	Albertarelli	Girowetz
Lops N. B.	Dorelli	Choris
Negri	Lazarini, (in the Pan-	Burny Dr.
Celestini	theon)	Hülmandel
Choris	Mazzanti	Graff
Benda	Morelli	Dittenhoffer
Mrs. Barthelemon and the daughter	Calcagni	Storace
	Croutsch	Arnold
Schinotti	Harrison	Barthelemon
Maffei [*bella, ma poco musica*]	Simoni	Schield *
	Miss Pool	Carter *
Capelletti	Miss Barck	Cramer
Davis (*detta Inglesina, la quale Recitava a Napoli quando l'aveva* 13 *anni ella è adesso vecchietta ma ha una buona scola*).	Mrs. Bland	Tomich
		Frike, No. 24
		Blandford-Street
		Manchester
		Square

Mad. Seconda *passabile*
Badini, poet.

Moravian. la Trobe dedicated his pianoforte sonatas to me.
Mazini at the pianoforte in the Panetheon.
Friderici
Burney Titschfield Street

Pianists.	Violinists.	Violoncellists.	Doctors.
Clementi	Salomon	Grosdill	Burney
Duschek	Cramer	Menel	Hess, in Oxford.
Girowetz	Clement, *petit*	Mara	Arnold
Diettenhofer	Barthelemon	Sperati	Dupuis, a great organist.
Burney	Schield	Scramb	
Mrs. Burney	Hindmarsb, Ingl.		

Pianists.	Violinists.
Hüllmandl	
Graff, also flautist	Scheener (Germ.)
Miss Barthelemon	Raimondi (Ital.)
Cramer	Serra of Marquis Durazzo
Miss Jansa.	
Humel, of Vienna	Borghi
	Giornowichi
Lenz, still very young.	Felix, Janievicz
	Jarowez
	Giardini

Two pages of one of the note books are filled with this list of singers, instrumentalists and composers in London. The added comments are as follows: "Maffei: Pretty, but a poor musician." "Davis, called the English woman, sang at Naples when she was thirteen years old. She is now old but she has a good school." "Madame Seconda, tolerable." Other remarks have been given in translation.

The "little" Clement was a boy violinist who grew into the famous artist for whom Beethoven wrote his violin concerto, who played it at sight at the rehearsal and at the revision of "Fidelio" at Prince Lichnowsky's house played the whole first violin part from memory.

Krumpholz, harpist. Mr. Blumb, imitated a

parrot and accompanied himself admirably on the pianoforte.

Mrs. de la Valle, a pupil of Krumpholz, plays not quite so well as Madame Krumpholz. Plays the pianoforte. Her sister-in-law plays the violin very nicely.

Mr. Antis, Bishop and a little *compositor*
Nicolai, Royal Chamberlain and *compositor*.

Hartman, flute player, had to leave England because of poverty, lost his wife by death, finally turned out a rascal.

On the 31st of December I was with Pleyl in the Pantheon. They played "La Pastorella Nobile" by Guglielmi. Madame Casentini played the first rôle and Lazarini, *primo huomo* (sic). The lean Calvesi *l'ultima parte*. The opera did not please; neither did the ballet despite the great Hillisbury.

Ambaschiador (Ambassador) the Count de Stadion.

Prince de Castelcicala, of Naples, the Marquis del Campo, of Spain.

My friend, you think I love you; in truth, you are not mistaken.

In solitude, too, there are divinely lovely duties, and to perform them in quiet is more than wealth.

HAYDN IN LONDON

Begehre nicht ein Glück zu gross
   Und nicht ein Weib zu schön;
Der Himmel möchte dir dies Loos
   Im Zorne zugestehn.

(Do not desire too great happiness or a too lovely wife. Heaven might, in anger, grant your wish!)

Wer mit Vernuft betracht' den Wechsel aller Sachen,
Den kan kein Glück nicht Froh, kein Unglück traurig machen.

(Who wisely observes the whirligig of things cannot be made happy by good fortune or unhappy by bad.)

Intra in gaudium habeo, et non habeor. Resurgam. In Coeloquies.

Chi ben commincia ha la meta dell' opera, ne si commincia ben se in dal cielo.

(An Italian form of "Well begun is half done.")

Gott im Herz, ein gut Weibchen im Arm,
Jenes macht selig, dieses ganz warm.

(God in one's heart, a good little wife in one's arm — the first brings salvation, the second warmth.)

With the warmth of genuine friendship I commend myself to you. This as a souvenir of —

Ken - ne Gott, die welt und

HIS NOTE BOOK

dich, lieb-ster Freund, und denk-an mich, und denk-an mich, Ken-ne Gott, die welt und dich, lieb-ster Freund.

The music is a canon in the octave, the second voice entering on the third beat of the third measure.

In 31 years 38,000 houses have been built in London.

Painters. Messrs. Ott and Guttenbrun.

On November 5 the boys celebrated the day on which the Guys set fire to the town.

Haydn has seen a celebration of Guy Fawkes' Day and is shaky in his history.

Kozwarra.

Beginning of May, 1792, Lord Barrymore gave a ball that cost 5,000 guineas. He paid 1,000 guineas for 1,000 peaches; 2,000 baskets of gooseberries cost 5 shillings apiece.

Prince of Wales's punch. — One bottle champagne, one bottle Burgundy, one bottle rum, ten lemons, two oranges, pound and a half of sugar.

On the 23^d of June, 1792, the Duchess of York gave a dinner under a tent in her garden for 180 persons. I saw it.

La risposta del S. Marchesi sopra una lettera del S. Gallini. Nell' anno 1791 ho ricevuto la sua gentilissima lettera. buona Notte.
Marchesi.

When a Quaker goes to Court he pays the doorkeeper to take his hat off for him; for a Quaker never doffs his hat to anybody. When the King's tax is to be paid an official enters his house and in his presence robs him of as much property as represents the tax in value. As the disguised thief is about to go out of the door with the goods the Quaker calls him back and asks: "How much money do you want for the stolen goods?" The official demands the amount of the tax, and in this way the Quaker pays the King's tax.

Anno 1791 the last great concert, with 885 persons, was held in Westminster. Anno 1792 it was transferred to St. Margaret's Chapel, with 200 performers. This evoked criticism.

HIS NOTE BOOK

Haydn refers here to the Handel Commemoration. The first of these gigantic affairs, as they were then considered, took place in Westminster Abbey in 1784. Haydn attended that of 1791, and was tremendously impressed by the grandeur of the performance. He had a good place near the King's box, and when the "Hallelujah Chorus" was sung he wept like a child and exclaimed, "He is the master of us all!"

On the 4th of August I went into the country twelve miles from London to visit the banker, Mr. Brassey, and remained five weeks. I was very well entertained. N. B. Mr. Brassey once cursed because he enjoyed too much happiness in this world.

In order to preserve milk for a long time take a bottle full of milk and place it in a vessel of earthenware or copper containing sufficient water to cover the bottle up to a little above the middle; then place it over a fire and let it boil half an hour. Take the bottle out and seal it so that no air may enter it. In this manner milk can be kept for many months. N. B. The bottle must be securely corked before it is put in the water. This was told me by a sea captain.

On March 26, at a concert by Mr. Barthelemon, an English *Pop* was present who fell into the profoundest melancholy on hearing the Andante:

etc.

because he had dreamed the night before that this Andante was a premonition of his death. He left the company at once and took to his bed. To-day, on April 25, I learned from Mr. Barthelemon that this evangelical priest had died.

The Andante is from the Symphony in D major, which is numbered 23 in the list of Breitkopf and Härtel. *Pop* is an Austrian colloquialism for priest. *Pop, Pabst, Pfaffe.* The concert was not Barthelemon's, but Miss Corri's, says Pohl.

On the 24th of 9 ber (November) I was invited by the Prince of Wales to visit his brother, the Duke of York, at Eatland (Oatlands). I remained two days and enjoyed many marks of graciousness and honor from the Prince of Wales as well as the Duchess, who is a daughter of the King of Prussia. The little castle, eighteen miles from London, lies upon an upland and commands a glorious view. Besides many beauties there is a remarkable grotto which cost £25,000 sterling. It took eleven years to build it. It is not very large and contains many diversions, and has flowing water from different

HIS NOTE BOOK

directions, a beautiful English garden, many entrances and exits, besides a neat bath. The Duke bought the property for £47,000 sterling. On the third day the Duke had me taken twelve miles toward town with his own horses. The Prince of Wales asked for my portrait. For two days we made music for four hours each evening, i. e., from 10 o'clock till two hours after midnight. Then we had supper, and at 3 o'clock we went to bed.

On the 30th I was three days in the country a hundred miles from London, with Sir Patric Blak (Patrick Blake). In going I passed the town of Cambridge, inspected all the universities, which are built conveniently in a row but separately. Each university has back of it a very roomy and beautiful garden, besides stone bridges, in order to afford passage over the stream which winds past. The King's Chapel is famous for its carvings. It is all of stone, but so delicate that nothing more beautiful could have been made of wood. It has endured already four hundred years, and everybody judges its age at about ten years, because of the firmness and peculiar whiteness of the stone. The students bear themselves like those at Oxford, but it is said they have better instructors. There are in all eight hundred students.

When two persons of opposite sexes love each other and receive permission to marry from the secular courts, the *Pop* is obliged to marry them as soon as they appear in church, even though they have loved against the wishes of their parents. If he does not the bridegroom and bride have the right as soon as he is out of the church to tear his robes off his body, and then the *Pop* is degraded and forever disqualified.

The obligation for 1000 florins deposited with Prince Esterhazi bears date July 10, 1791.

Covent garden is the National Theatre. On the 10th of December I attended the opera called "The Woodman." It was on the day that the life story of Madam Bilington, good and bad, had been announced. Such impertinent enterprises are generally undertaken for selfish interests. She sang timidly this evening but very well. The first tenor has a good voice and a fairly good style, but he uses the falsetto to excess. He sang a trill on high C and ran up to G. The second tenor tried to imitate him but could not make the change from the natural voice to the falsetto; besides he is very unmusical. He creates a new tempo, now $3/4$ then $2/4$ and cuts his phrases wherever he pleases. But the orchestra is used to him. The leader is Mr. Baumgartner, a German, who, however, has almost forgotten his mother-tongue. The theatre is very dark and dirty, about as large as the Vienna Court Theatre. The common herd in the galleries, as is the case in all theatres, is very impertinent. It gives the pitch in a boisterous manner and the performers are obliged to repeat according to its noisy wishes. The parterre and all the boxes frequently have to applaud a great deal to secure a repetition, but they succeeded this evening with the duet in the third act which is very beautiful. The controversy lasted nearly a quarter of an hour before parterre and boxes triumphed and the duo was repeated. The two performers stood in a fright on the stage, now retiring then again coming to the front. *The orchestra is sleepy.*

Mozard (sic) died the 5th day of December, 1791.

Mozart had been among the last to say farewell to Haydn when he left Vienna in company with Salomon, who had engaged him for the London season, on December 15, 1790. Salomon had planned a visit also for Mozart, who had not been to London since he had astounded the English aristocracy with his prodigious talents in 1764–'65. But when the two friends shook hands at parting Mozart said: " This is probably our last farewell in this life." And his premonition was fulfilled. Haydn, who was born twenty-four years earlier than Mozart, died eighteen years later.

HAYDN IN LONDON

Pleyl came to London on the 23ᵈ of December. On the 24ᵗʰ I dined with him.

Ignaz Pleyel, a pupil of Haydn, had been brought to London by the managers of the so-called Professional Concerts, which were given in opposition to those of Salomon for which Haydn had come. The rivalry between the concert organizations was very bitter and a newspaper article which told that negotiations had been begun with Pleyel, said that Haydn was too old, weak and exhausted to produce new music; wherefore he only repeated himself in his compositions. The friendship of master and pupil was undisturbed by the unseemly wrangle.

Haymarket Theatre. It will hold 4,000 persons; the pit, or parterre, alone holds 1,200, and ten persons can sit comfortably in each box. The " Amphy Theater " is round, four stories high and to light it a beautiful large chandelier, with seventy lights hangs suspended from the ceiling in the middle. It illuminates the entire house. But there are *a parte* small lusters in the first and second stories, which are fastened to the boxes.

I had to pay one and a half guineas for the bell peals at Oxforth when I received the doctor's degree, and half a guinea for the robe. The journey cost six guineas.

HIS NOTE BOOK

It was on July 8, 1791, that Haydn received the degree of Doctor of Music, *honoris causa*, from Oxford University. His thesis was the so-called Oxford symphony, and after the ceremony he sent a canon cancrizans a tre, set to the words, "Thy Voice, O Harmony, is divine," to the University.

The city of London has 4,000 carts for cleaning the streets, of which 2,000 work every day.

On the 17th of March 1792, I was bled in London.

In the month of August I journeyed at noon in an East India merchantman with six cannon. I was gloriously entertained. In this month, too, I went with Mr. Fraser on the Thames from Westminster Bridge to Richmond, where we had dinner on an island. We were twenty-four persons and a band of music. In England a large war vessel is reckoned according to the number of its cannons. Each cannon is estimated at 1,000 pounds.

Mme. Mara was hissed (*ausgeklatscht*) at Oxford because she did not rise from her seat when the Hallelujah chorus was sung.

On the 14th of December I dined for the first time at the house of Mr. Shaw. He received me below stairs at the door, and conducted me thence to his wife, who was surrounded by her two daughters and other ladies. While I was bowing all around I suddenly perceived that the lady of the house, besides her daughters and the other ladies, wore on their headdresses a pearl-colored band, of three-fingers' breadth, embroidered in gold with the name of Haydn, and Mr. Shaw wore the name on the two ends of his collar in the finest steel beads. The coat was of the finest cloth, smooth, and bore beautiful steel buttons. The mistress is the most beautiful woman I ever saw. N. B. — Her husband wanted me to give him a souvenir, and I gave him a tobacco-box which I had just bought for a guinea. He gave me his in exchange. A few days afterward I visited him and found that he had had a case of silver put over the box I had given him, on the cover of which was engraved Apollo's harp, and round it the words *Ex dono celeberrimi Josephi Haydn.* N. B. — The mistress gave me a stick-pin as a souvenir.

At the first concert the Adagio of the symphony in D was repeated.

At the second concert the chorus and the above symphony were repeated; .also the first Allegro and the Adagio.

In the third concert the new symphony in B-flat was played and the first and last Allegros were "encort."

HIS NOTE BOOK

Haydn's first three concerts were given on March 11th, 18th and 25th, 1791. The new symphonies which Haydn brought forward in agreement with his contract with Salomon, were Nos. 2 and 4 of the so-called Salomon set. Haydn conducted seated at the harpsichord, as was the custom at the time. Salomon led the orchestra which numbered about forty men, twelve to sixteen being violinists.

Lord Clermont (Claremont) once gave a large supper, and when the health of the King was drunk he ordered the brass band to play the familiar song " God save the King " in the street in the midst of a terrible snowstorm. This happened on February 19, 1792, so madly do they carry on in England.

The chapel at Windsor is a very old but splendid building. The high altar cost 50,000 florins. It is the ascension of Christ in stained glass. This year, 1792, a Christ appearing to the Shepherds was made for the side altar at the right, and this small one is valued higher than the large one. The view from the terrace is divine.

Hardy, Otto, Guttenbrun, Hoppner, Dassie.
The first four gentlemen painted my portrait. Dassie in wax.

The Theatre of Varieties Amusantes in Saville Row. — On the 13th of November I was invited

HAYDN IN LONDON

there. It is a marionet play. The figures were well directed, the singers bad, but the orchestra pretty good.

Before her departure for Italy Mara sang four times at the Haymarket Theatre in Dr. Arne's opera "Artaserses." She won great applause, and was paid 100£ for each performance.

The larger traveller's lead pencil cost 1½ guineas.

		shilling.	penz.
The small		5	6
The pen		6	6
		shilling	penc.
Stel buttons	2 £	2	0
a steel girdle	1	4	0
a steel chain	1	11	6
2 secisars (scissors)			
3 sh. each		6	
3 at 6 sh. each		18	0
1 at		7	6
1 at	1	9	0
1 Penn Knifes		1	0

This memorandum, obviously a list of trinkets designed as gifts for his friends at home, is in English, barring the first two items.

On November 9th, 1791 sent to Mr. v. Kees, two symphonies *per postum* for which I paid

HIS NOTE BOOK

1 guinea 11½ shillings, and 3 shillings for 2 letters and, for copying, 1 guinea.

Noyan, a drink composed of nutmeg, rum and sugar. It comes from Martinique, West Indies, which belongs to France.

Oranges come from Portugal in the middle of November, but they are pale and not so good as they are later.

On the 5th of December there was a fog so thick that one might have spread it on bread. In order to write I had to light a candle as early as 11 o'clock.

English Fanaticism. — Miss Dora Jordan, a mistress of the Duke of Clarens (Clarence) and the best actress in Drury Lane, one evening when she was expected to play wrote to the impresario an hour before the beginning of the comedy that she had suddenly become ill and therefore could not act. When the curtain was raised in order to inform the public of the fact and to state a willingness to give another spectacle the whole house began to howl, demanding an immediate performance of the comedy which had been announced, with another actress to read the rôle of the Jordan. This was objected to, but the public became stubborn and had to be satisfied in its way. Miss Jordan gained the contempt of the public because she openly drove in Hey (Hyde) Park with the

Duke but without shoes. But she begged for pardon in all the newspapers, and was wholly forgiven.

A gang of rowdies bawled this song, yelling so that one could hear them 1000 paces away from the street in every nook and cranny.

Mr. Bressy, No. 71 Lombard Street.

II

HIS ENGLISH LOVE

THE existence of a batch of love letters written to Haydn during his visits to London has been known to students ever since Dies's little biography of the composer appeared in Vienna in 1810. C. F. Pohl devotes several pages of his fascinating book, "Haydn in London" to them, and reprints a few passages from them; but the letters themselves do not appear to have been printed either in their original English or a German translation until I gave them to the world through the columns of "The New York Tribune." I was enabled to do so through coming into possession of the note books described in the last chapter. Haydn had copied them out in full, a proceeding which tells its own story touching his feelings toward the missives and their fair author — for she was fair. Fourteen years after they had been received they were still treasured by the composer among his souvenirs of the English visit. To Dies, who asked him about them, Haydn answered, with a twinkle in his gray eyes: "They are letters from an English widow in London who loved me. Though sixty years old, she was still lovely and amiable, and I should in all likelihood have married her if I had been single."

Alas for the lovely and amiable correspondent, there was a Mistress Haydn at home in Vienna, who still grappled the dear old man (he was fifty-nine) to her person, if not to her soul, with hoops of the law! Mistress Haydn was neither lovely nor amiable. Had she been either, or both, it is not likely that Papa's heart would so easily have become errant, though he was, as he himself confessed, fond of looking at pretty women. *Frau Doktorin*, moreover, was a Xantippe. That she proved even while Mistress Schroeter was laying siege to Dr. Haydn's heart. Shortly before Haydn started for home, in 1792, he received a letter from his wife asking for two thousand florins out of his earnings to pay for a house which she wished to purchase in the suburb of Vienna now called Gumpendorf. It is the house known as No. 19 Haydngasse, to which a marble memorial tablet was affixed in 1840. In the letter asking for the purchase money the amiable lady described the house as just the thing for her to "live in as a widow." Papa Haydn did not send the money, but on his return he looked at the house, and, finding it pleasantly situated and to his taste, bought it. Xantippe died seven years later, "and now," said Haydn, telling the story in 1806, "I'm living in it as a widower."

And who was she whom Marjorie Fleming, Sir Walter's "wifie," would have called Haydn's "loveress?" The note books yield up part of the secret:

Mistress Schroeter, No. 6 James-st., Buckingham's Gate.

The musical encyclopædists have done the rest. True, she shines in the books only by reflected light, but you may read of her in Sir George Grove's "Dictionary of Music and Musicians," Fétis's "Biographie Universelle des Musiciens," "Rees's Encyclopedia" and in lesser handbooks, so you look under the name Johann Samuel Schroeter. This Schroeter was an excellent musician, who came to London in 1772 and ten years later succeeded "the English Bach" as music-master to the Queen. He was one of the first musicians to disclose the possibilities of the pianoforte as distinguished from the harpsichord, and his talents were highly appreciated in professional as well as Court circles.

HAYDN IN LONDON

He came of a talented family. His father was oboist of the royal orchestra at Warsaw, his brother Johann Heinrich was a violinist, and his sister Corona Elizabeth Wilhelmine was the singer, actress, composer and painter, whose portrait still hangs in the Grand Ducal library at Weimar, where it was placed by Goethe, as may be read in a later chapter of this volume.

As for the lady in the case, let two excerpts from the books suffice. Dr. Burney, writing of Johann Samuel Schroeter in "Rees's Encyclopedia," said:

He married a young lady of considerable fortune, who was his scholar, and was in easy circumstances; but there was a languor discoverable in his looks while disease was preying upon him several years before his decease.

Fétis says in his "Biographie Universelle des Musiciens":

Un mariage clandestin avec une de ses élèves, dont la famille appertenait à la haute société, lui suscita beaucoup de chagrin. La menace d'être traduit devant la cour de la chancellerie l'obliga de consentir à l'annulation de son hymen, moyennant une pension viagère de 500 livres sterling. L'éclat qu' avait en cette affaire lui fit chercher une retraite à la campagne.

HIS ENGLISH LOVE

He died in 1788 — three years before Haydn came to London. The widow must have made Haydn's acquaintance soon after his arrival in town, and become his pupil, for on June 29, 1791, she writes to him as follows:

Mrs. Schroeter presents her compliments to Mr. Haydn and informs him she is just returned to town and will be very happy to see him whenever it is convenient to him to give her a lesson.

James-st., Buckingham gate, Wednesday, June the 29th, 1791.

Unless Haydn was fibbing it a bit for the sake of appearances, it is probable that Dies misunderstood his remark about the age of the lady when she wrote the letters. She may have been sixty years old when Haydn told the story in 1806, but it is wholly improbable that she was that age in 1792. Dr. Burney, who knew her in all likelihood, speaks of her as "a young lady" when she was married to Schroeter, who was only thirty-eight years old when he died. If she was sixty years old when Haydn met her, she must have been eighteen years her husband's senior, and could not well be described as a "young" lady.

In 1794, when Haydn returned to London for a second visit, he did not move into his

HAYDN IN LONDON

old lodgings, but found others at No. 1 Bury-st., St. James's.

This much more pleasantly situated dwelling, says Pohl, he probably owed to the considerate care of Mrs. Schroeter, who, by the same token, thus brought him nearer to herself. A short and pleasant walk of scarcely ten minutes through St. James's Palace and the Mall (a broad alley alongside of St. James's Park) led him to Buckingham Palace, and near at hand was the house of Mrs. Schroeter. When he went away from London forever he left behind him the scores of his six last symphonies " in the hands of a lady," ·probably Mrs. Schroeter.

Finally, let it be added that Haydn honored the lady by inscribing three trios to her, Nos. 1, 2 and 6 in the Breitkopf and Härtel list.

The letters were copied into one of the two note books by Haydn without regard to chronological sequence; the following arrangement is my own, three undated letters being put at the end, though they obviously ought to be early in the list. The abbreviations are easily understood, and, indeed, find their explanation sooner or later in the letters themselves. " M. D." is my dear; " M. Dst.," my dearest; " M. L.," my love; " H." and " Hn.," Haydn.

HIS ENGLISH LOVE

Wednesday, Febr. 8th, 1792.

M. D. Inclos'd I have sent you the words of the song you desire. I wish much to know *how you do* today. I am very sorry to lose the pleasure of seeing you this morning, but I hope you will have time to come tomorrow. I beg my D you will take great care of your health and do not fatigue yourself with too much application to business. My thoughts and best wishes are always with you, and I ever am with the utmost sincerity M. D. your &c

March the 7th 92.

My D. I was extremely sorry to part with you so suddenly last night. our conversation was particularly interesting and I had a thousand affectionate things to Say to you. my heart was and is full of *tenderness* for you. but no language can express *half* the *Love* and *Affection* I feel for you. you are *dearer* to me *every Day* of my life. I am very Sorry I was so dull and Stupid yesterday, indeed my *Dearest* it was nothing but my being indisposed with a cold occasion'd my Stupidity. I thank you a thousand times for your Concern for me. I am truly Sensible of your goodness and I assure you my D. if anything had happened to trouble me, I wou'd have open'd my heart and told you with the greatest confidence. oh, how earnestly I wish to See you. I hope you will come to me tomorrow. I shall be happy to See you both in the Morning and the Evening. God Bless you my love. my thoughts and best wishes ever accompany you and I always am with the most Sincere and invariable Regard my D

Your truly affectionate ——
my Dearest I cannot be
happy till I see you if
you Know do tell me
when you will come.

My D. I am extremely sorry I can not have the pleasure of seeing you to morrow as I am going to Blackheath. if you are not engaged this Evening I should be very happy if you will do me the favor to come to me — and I hope to have the happiness to See you on Saturday to dinner. my thoughts and tenderest affections are always with you and I ever am most truly my D your Faithful &c.

April 4th 92.

My D: With this you will receive the Soap. I beg you a thousand Pardons for not sending it sooner. I know you will have the goodness to excuse me. I hope to hear you are quite well and have Slept well — I shall be happy to See you my D: as soon as possible. I shall be much obliged to you if you will do me the favor to send me Twelve Tikets for your Concert. may all *success*

attend you my *ever* D H that Night and always is the sincere and hearty wish of your
                    Invariable and Truly affectionate
James St. April 8th 1792

James St. Thursday, April 12th
   M. D.
   I am so *truly anxious* about *you*. I must write to beg to know *how you do?* I was very sorry I *had* not the pleasure of Seeing you this Evening, my thoughts have been *constantly* with you and indeed my D. L. no words can express half the tenderness and *affection I feel for you*. I thought you seemed out of Spirits this morning. I wish I could always remove every trouble from your mind. be assured my D: I partake with the most perfect sympathy in *all your sensations* and my regard for you is *Stronger every day*. my best wishes always attend you and I am ever my D. H. most sincerely your Faithful etc.

   M. D. I was extremely Sorry to hear this morning that you were indisposed. I am told you were five hours at your Studys yesterday. indeed *my D. L.* I am afraid it will hurt you. why shou'd you who have already produced So many *wonderful* and *Charming* compositions Still fatigue yourself with Such close application. I almost tremble for your health let me prevail on you my *much-loved* H. not to keep to your Studys so long at *one time*. my D love if you cou'd know how very precious your welfare is to me I flatter myself you wou'd endeaver to preserve it for my sake as well as *your own*. pray inform me how you do and how you have Slept. I hope to see you to Morrow at the concert and on Saturday I shall be happy to See you here to dinner. in the mean time my D: my Sincerest good wishes constantly attend you and I ever am with the *tenderest* regard your most &c

J. S. April the 19th 92

April 24th 1792.

My D. I cannot leave London without Sending you a line to assure you my thoughts, my best wishes and tenderest affections will inseparably attend you till we meet again. the Bearer will also deliver you the March. I am very Sorry I could not write it Sooner, nor better, but I hope my D. you will excuse it, and if it is not passable I will send you the *Dear* original directly. If my H. would employ me oftener to write Music I hope I should improve and I Know I should delight in the occupation. now my D. L. let me intreat you to take the greatest care of your *health*. I hope to see you Friday at the concert and on Saturday to dinner, till when and ever I most sincerely am and Shall be yours etc.

M. D. I am very anxious to Know *how you do*, and hope to hear you have been in good health ever Since I Saw you. as the time for your charming Concert advances I feel my Self more and

HIS ENGLISH LOVE

more interested for your Success, and heartily *wish* everything may turn out to your Satisfaction. do me the favor to send me six Tickets more. on Saturday my D. L. I hope to see you to dinner. in the mean time my thoughts my best wishes and tenderest affections constantly attend you and I ever am my D. H. most sincerely and aff.

   J. S.   May ye 2^d 1792

                 James St. Tuesday May the 8th

  My Dst I am extremely Sorry I have not the pleasure Seeing you to Day, but hope to see you to Morrow at one o'Clock and if you can take your *Dinner* with me to Morrow I shall be very glad. I hope to See you also on thursday to dinner, but I Suppose you will be obliged to go to the concert that Evening and you Know the other concert is on Friday and you go to the country on Saturday, this my *Dst Love* makes me more Solicitous for you to Stay with me to Morrow, if you are not engaged, as I wish to have as much of your company as *possible*. God Bless you my D. H. I always am with the tenderest Regard your sincere and affectionate ———

  May 17th.

  M. D. Permit me to return you a thousand thanks for this Evening's entertainment. Where *your sweet* compositions and your excellent performance combine, it cannot fail of being the most *charming concert* but independent of that the pleasure of *Seeing you* must ever give me infinite Satisfaction. Pray inform me *how you do?* and if you have *Slept well?* I hope to See you to morrow my *D.* and on Saturday to dinner, till when and always I remain most sincerely my D. L. most Faithfully etc.

M. D. If you will do me the favor to take your dinner with me tomorrow I shall be very happy to see you and I *particularly* wish for the pleasure of *your* company my *Dst Love before* our other friends come. I hope to hear you are in *-good Health*. My best wishes and tenderest Regards are your constant attendants and I *ever* am with the *firmest* Attachment my Dst H most sincerely and Affectionately yours R. S.

James S. Tuesday Ev. May 22ᵈ.

My Dst. I beg to know *how you do?* I hope to hear your head-ach is *entirely gone* and that you have *Slept well.* I shall be very very happy to See you on Sunday any time convenient to you after one o'Clock. I hope to see you my D. Lᵉ on tuesday as usual to Dinner, and I Shall be much obliged to you if you will inform me what Day will be agreeable to you to meet Mr. *Mtris.* and *Miss Stone* at my house to Dinner. I should be glad if it was either Thursday or Friday, whichever Day *you please* to fix. I will send to Mr. Stone to let them know. I long to see you my Dst H. let me have that pleasure as soon as you can till when

and Ever I remain with the *firmest* attachment My Dst L.
Most faithfully and affectionately yours——
Friday June ye 1st 1792

M. D. I can not close my eyes to sleep till I have return'd you ten thousand thanks for the inexpressible delight I have received from *your ever Enchanting* compositions and your *incomparably Charming* performance of them. be assured my D. H. that among *all* your numerous admirers no one has listened with more profound attention and no one can have Such high veneration for your most *brilliant Talents* as I *have*. indeed my D. L. no tongue *can express* the gratitude I *feel* for the infinite pleasure your Musick has given me. accept then my repeeted thanks for it and let me also assure you with heart felt affection that I Shall ever consider the happiness of your acquaintance as one of the *Chief* Blessings of my life, and it is the *Sincer* wish of my heart to preserve to cultivate and to merit it more and more. I hope to hear you are quite well. Shall be happy to see you to dinner and if you *can* come at three o'Clock it would give me a great pleasure as I shou'd be particularly glad to see you my D. befor the rest of our friends come. God Bless you my h: I ever am with the firmest and most perfect attachment your &c.
Wednesday night, June the 6th 1792.

HAYDN IN LONDON

My Dst Inclosed I send you the verses you was so Kind as to lend me and am very much obliged to you for permitting me to take a copy of them. pray inform me *how you do*, and let me know my *Dst L* when you will dine with me; I shall be *happy* to *See* you to dinner either tomorrow or tuesday whichever is most Convenient to you. I am *truly anxious* and *impatient* to *See you* and I wish to have as much of *your company* as possible; indeed *my Dst H*. I *feel* for *you* the *fondest* and *tenderest* affection the human Heart is capable of and I ever am with the *firmest* attachment my Dst Love

most Sincerely, Faithfully
and most affectionately yours

Sunday Evening, June 10, 1792

My Dearest.

I hope to hear you are in good *Health* and have had an *agreeable* Journey, that you have been much *amused* with the Race and that *everything* has turned out to your *satisfaction*. Pray my *Dst love* inform me how *you* do? *Every* circumstance concerning you *my beloved* H^d is *interesting* to me. I shall be *very happy* to *see* you to *dinner tomorrow* and I *ever* am with the sincerest and *tenderest Regard my* Dst Hn most Faithfully and affectionately yours

R. S.

James S. Thursday Even. June ye 14th 1792

HIS ENGLISH LOVE

My D. I hope to hear you are in good *health* and that you *Slept well* last night. I shall be very happy to see you on Monday morning — permit me to remind you about Mr. Frasers and you will be so good as to let me know on Monday how it is Settled. God Bless you my D Love, my thoughts and best wishes are your constant attendants, and I ever am with the tenderest Regard my D. H. most etc.

June ye 26th 92

M. D.

I was *extremely sorry* I had not the pleasure of *seeing you to-day*, indeed my Dst Love it was a very great disappointment to me as every moment of your company is *more* and *more precious* to me now your *departure* is so near. I hope to hear you are *quite well* and I shall be very happy to see you my Dst Hn. any time to-morrow after one o'clock, if you can come; but if not I shall hope for the pleasure of Seeing *you* on *Monday*. You will receive this letter to-morrow morning. I would not send it to-day for fear you should not be at home and I *wish* to have your answer. God Bless you my Dst Love, once more I repeat let me See you as *Soon* as possible. I *ever* am with the most *inviolable attachment* my Dst and most beloved H.

most faithfully and most
affectionately yours
R. S.

HAYDN IN LONDON

June the 26th, 1792.

My Dearest.

I am quite impatient to know how you do this Morning and if you Slept well last Night. I am much obliged to you for all your Kindness yesterday, and heartily thank you for it. I earnestly *long* to see you my Dst L: and I hope to have that pleasure *this morning*. My *Thoughts* and best *Regards* are incessantly with you, and I ever am my D. H.

most faithfully and most affectionately your ——

M. D.

I was extremely sorry I had not the pleasure of *your* company *this morning* as I most *anxiously wish'd* to See you — my *thoughts* are continually with you my beloved H: and my *affection* for you *increases daily*, no words can express half the *tender Regard* I feel for you. I hope my Dst L: I shall have the happiness of Seeing you to-morrow to dinner in the meantime my best wishes always attend you, and I *ever* am with the *firmest* attachment my D. H. most etc.

M. D.

I am heartily sorry I was so unfortunate not to See you when you call'd on me this morning. Can you my D. be so good as to dine with me to-day? I beg you will if it is possible. You cannot imagine how miserable I am that I did not

HIS ENGLISH LOVE

See you. do come to-Day I intreat you. I always am M. D. with the tenderest Regard etc.
Monday, 2 o'clock.

I am just returned from the concert where I was very much Charmed with your *delightful* and enchanting *Compositions* and your Spirited and interesting performance of them. accept ten thousand thanks for the great pleasure I *always* receive from your *incomparable* Music. My D : I intreat you to inform me how you do and if you get any *Sleep* to Night. I am *extremely anxious* about your health. I hope to hear a good account of it. god Bless you my H : come to me to-morrow. I shall be happy to See you both morning and Evening. I always am with the tenderest Regard my D : your Faithful and Affectionate
Friday Night, 12 o'clock.

A MOZART CENTENARY

I

SOCIAL AND ARTISTIC SALZBURG

To the ordinary summer tourist Salzburg is the gateway to the Salzkammergut. To the music lover it is the birthplace of Mozart. From the fifteenth to the eighteenth of July, 1891, inclusive, it was lifted into extraordinary prominence by the latter circumstance. Save those lent her by her greatest son the city has few opportunities to cull out a holiday, so it was but natural that the centenary of his death should be remembered as the centenary of his birth had been. But Mozart died in December, a most inhospitable season in the latitude of Salzburg, and one when the strangers within the city's gates might easily be counted on the fingers of a single landlord. I fancy that when the project of celebrating the hundredth anniversary of the great composer's death was first mooted in 1891, there was scarcely a citizen in the town outside of the teachers and pupils of the Mozarteum, who would not have gladly sacrificed "Requiem" and "Zauberflöte" to have had Mozart die in July or August instead of December; but since that was something beyond their control, and no one was willing to lose the advantages of a midsummer celebration, resort was had to a sentimental fiction and the festival was moved forward six months.

The fact that the week chosen was that immediately preceding the opening of the Wagner festival at Bayreuth was calculated to give an artistic significance to the celebration which I wish I could persuade myself had entered the thoughts of the Committee of Arrangements. It disposed the thoughtful to reflect on the changes which have come over dramatic music within the time bounded by the archonships of Mozart and Wagner. Progress or retrogression — which is it? He would be a brave man, or a careless one, who would dare to assert the latter, yet I am bound to say that even the most ardent admirers of Wagner who came to Salzburg on their way to Bayreuth must have felt a strange swelling of the heart during the Mozart festival which may have been matched in degree but scarcely in kind when a week later the harmonies began to ascend like clouds of incense from the mystical

SOCIAL AND ARTISTIC SALZBURG

abyss in the temple of the oracle of Bayreuth. Unhappily, however, for the good opinion which we all like to hold with reference to those who contribute to the happiness of mankind by arranging great festivals, I fear that the Committee of the Mozart centenary if they thought of the Bayreuth festival at all, thought of it only as an affair which might help them in the financial part of their enterprise; visitors to Bayreuth — a term that now includes practically the whole peripatetic company in Europe — might easily be persuaded to make Salzburg a temporary way-station. Thus the master of the present would seem to pay tribute to the master of the past, and the mingling of the disciples of both would encourage the inn-keepers of Salzburg in the good opinion of Mozart which it is their duty to maintain.

In the middle of the eighteenth century Salzburg was the seat of a principality whose sovereign wielded a two-fold and doubly despotic power by reason of his headship in both church and state. I needed only to glance out of my hotel window across the rushing Salzach to see monuments of that power. The old fortress Hohensalzburg frowns down on the town from its dominating height; the cathedral lifts its towers with Roman haughtiness amidst the houses huddled together below. All week long the walls of the houses showed a festive countenance and glowed with a gay irruption of patriotic bunting, while castle and church preserved an aspect of stern severity. It was as though the spirit of that brutal Prince-Archbishop, who a little more than a hundred years before had thrown away the most priceless jewel in his diadem, was still abroad. There seemed to be a peculiar propriety in the grim indifference of the fortress to the festival and the perfunctory part played by the cathedral. The hand which wielded temporal power in Salzburg a century before was never extended in helpful kindness to her child of genius, and when it was extended in episcopal benediction in the cathedral none knew better than Mozart that it symbolized a mockery and a lie. The archbishop who on the first day of the festival performed just enough of a liturgical function to permit it to be opened with a performance of Mozart's "Requiem" was a prelate merely — long ago the last shred of temporal power was stripped from one of his predecessors — but he was yet Archbishop of Salzburg, and to a devotee of Mozart that title has a sound of evil omen. So, at the

SOCIAL AND ARTISTIC SALZBURG

outset, it was gratifying to note that the festive spirit of the great assemblage changed the religious function into a secular celebration, and the soul of Mozart was not vexed but left in the care of its lovers. To them a truer sanctuary than the cathedral was the humble house in the Getreide Gasse where Mozart was born.

The celebration was not only secular — it was democratic as well. A Grand Duke of Austria, the youngest brother of the Emperor, was in attendance in an official capacity, but there was not one of the artists who took part in the musical features of the commemoration who was not a greater object of interest to the people than he. In simple truth I fear that he was sadly bored by the exercises, but it must be said to his credit that he performed his function (which was to lend his presence to the occasion and be seen by those who wished to see him) with entire gravity. His sharp features (an Austrian Grand Duke is so thin that he rarely feels the wind) never reflected the slightest interest in the proceedings, but neither did they betray the fact that he was offering himself as a living sacrifice to duty. A pretty American girl filled his lorgnette for full five minutes at the theatre when, on the last night of the festival, "The Marriage of Figaro" was played, and he exhibited a comical desire to use his opera-glasses at extremely short range on a few other persons, but beyond this he had nothing to do with the celebration nor it with him. It was a people's tribute to the memory of one who came from the people.

I am still lost in amazement at the fact that the festival was actually carried out on the lines laid down by the Committee of Arrangements, and came to 'a satisfactory conclusion instead of falling hopelessly to pieces. Only the easy-going disposition of the Austrian people and the lack of interest on the part of foreigners made this possible. The festival, fortunately, had not been widely announced. Had even a small fraction of the tourists who a week later flocked to Bayreuth, come it would have been impossible to accommodate them at the musical features of the celebration. A splendid programme of these features had been arranged: A performance of the "Requiem;" two concerts by the Philharmonic Society of Vienna under Wilhelm Jahn, at the time Director of the Imperial Court Opera; finally a representation of "The Marriage of Figaro." At all of these entertainments the purchaser of

SOCIAL AND ARTISTIC SALZBURG

a general ticket costing fourteen Gulden (less than six dollars) was entitled to a reserved seat. The cathedral in which the "Requiem" was sung is said to have seating and standing room for ten thousand persons; the theatre, in which the opera was given, seats three hundred and fifty, and under such pressure as it was subjected to afforded standing-room for one hundred more. Any committee, except one composed of citizens of Salzburg, might easily have quailed before the problem raised by such a discrepancy. The world had been invited (not very loudly or urgently, but still invited) to participate in the celebration. No trouble about the "Requiem," but how about the opera and the concerts which took place in the Aula Academica, a hall with a seating capacity of twelve hundred or so? Evidently the committee knew the character of their townspeople and the majority of the visitors who were likely to come. The mass would be satisfied with the popular and spectacular elements in the celebration. When it was possible to hear the "Requiem" and see a torchlight procession for nothing and enjoy a fête in the garden of the Mirabellschloss, where beer would be plentiful at regular rates and the music and illuminations free, the committee knew that they would not be greatly distressed by demands for tickets for the other features of the festival. Of course many came who could not be accommodated at the concerts, and there were many, many more who could not hope to get inside the tiny box of a theatre; but these were simply told that the seats were pre-empted. "Sorry; but we have only three hundred and fifty seats in the theatre. Should a ticket be returned it will be at your disposal, otherwise — *ich habe die Ehre*" — and the applicant was disposed of. Yet no one complained. It was the most astonishing exhibition of good nature that ever fell under my notice.

"You will be astonished at other phases of that good nature before you get out of Austria," said a Scotch friend at the hotel. "You ask how this people can endure to reflect upon the fact that they appear to every foreign visitor in the attitude of a beggar asking alms. Why, bless your innocent soul, they don't reflect upon it! It wouldn't do. They must perforce be *gleichgiltig* to keep up with the procession. They are thoughtless and merry of terrible necessity. If an Austrian officer of sensibilities were to stop to reflect upon the condition of

SOCIAL AND ARTISTIC SALZBURG

his country he would have to blow out his brains. So we all, who live in Vienna, grow frivolous and careless, and when we order a bite to eat we tip the head-waiter who collects the bill, tip the waiter who serves the viands, tip the waiter who brings the beer and tip the waiter who sells the cigars; and after we have been here long enough to have become sufficiently imbued with the national feeling we tip the street-car conductor for allowing us the privilege of paying him the legal fare — we give him two Kreutzer for collecting eight."

It was nip and tuck for some hours, whether or not, I who had come all the way from New York to attend the festival should hear the concerts and opera at all. If a thrifty soul had not changed his mind and returned his ticket to be resold I should have been turned away by the committee with: "I am sorry, but — *ich habe die Ehre,*" and then have been expected to be merry over it, or been invited to hear the "Requiem" standing up for nothing and mingle with the crowd at the garden fête at an expense of twenty cents, see lights and drink beer for the greater glory of Mozart. Even after I had secured my tickets and certificates I was denied the pleasure of exhibiting them to the door-keepers. A badge which I wore on the lapel of my coat was as potent as the storied "open, sesame" in the robbers' cave. I had bought it for eighty Kreutzer at a book-shop; afterwards I was told that it was one of a kind only sold to festival subscribers.

Every feature of the business management of the affair was incomprehensible. Except with the hotel people I never saw money play so insignificant a rôle. The artists all gave their services gratuitously. Ninety-two members of the Vienna Philharmonic Society endured a railway trip of fourteen hours, played at two public rehearsals and two concerts, and asked nothing, not even seats at the theatre, for their labor. Then, as if that were not enough, a score of them walked through a drenching rain in the torchlight procession. Madame Essipoff and the singers at the concerts and opera were equally generous. Frau Wilt broke a three years' silence to accept the invitation of the committee and sing an air in which she once was famous. For the sake of my ears I wish that she had been stouter in her determination to remain in retirement, but I feel bound to record so striking an instance of the ideality which marked the artistic side of the festival. It was all lovely, and from

SOCIAL AND ARTISTIC SALZBURG

a social and artistic point of view the affair seemed to be pervaded by that spirit of amiability which was the ingredient most generously present in Mozart's character.

It was a commemorative celebration of Mozart's death, but only a few could have suspected it. Only the "Requiem," a beautiful musical reminiscence with which Director Hummel introduced the Viennese actor who read the epilogue of the festival (which was at the same time a prologue to "The Marriage of Figaro") and some words in the official addresses drew attention to that fact. I have said that the festive spirit of the populace prevented the "Requiem" from appearing as a solemn religious function as had been designed. I fear that Director Hummel's device also missed its aim with the audience in the theatre, because of its subtlety. Yet it was a most gracious device. Just before the curtain rose to enable the actor to speak the lines written by Freiherr von Berger, of Vienna, the orchestra, at a sign from Director Hummel, played a few measures of the *Lacrymosa* from the master's mass for the dead. They were the last strains which Mozart's mortal ears had caught up. The story of his death is a familiar one. He died while those about his bed were singing parts of his uncompleted "Requiem." He had sung along but his voice failed him in the *Lacrymosa*, and his last gesture was a hint to his pupil Süssmayr, touching an effect which he wished to have introduced in the instrumental part of his swan-song. It was necessary to know this incident to appreciate the pathetic beauty of the few measures abruptly broken off on the entrance of the speaker with which the solemn features of the commemoration came to an end. They borrowed a significance from the concluding lines of the epilogue, but also lent a meaning and tenderness to them which I shall not undertake to describe. Translated with regard to the sentiment rather than the music of the poet's verses those lines read as follows:

But what a death! The singer of life's fulness,
Rapt in an ecstasy, list'ning in awe to tones
Which, messengers from another world, proclaim'd
The silent mystery of death,
Invoked Apollo, bearer of the lyre and bow,
To send him tones for his last masterpiece
Such as no mortal ears had ever heard.
Lost in deep listening, the god reached out
An errant hand; took up the bow
Where he had meant the tuneful lyre,
And sent an arrow to the heart,
The swelling, list'ning heart, of the rapt singer.

SOCIAL AND ARTISTIC SALZBURG

Not infinite melody, but infinite stillness then
Fell tenderly upon th' expectant brow.
And when they pressed his eyelids down,
There hung upon his lashes still a tear,
The last, the hottest he had ever wept,
In contemplation of his work,
The sweetest, strangest miracle
That he himself had wrought.
Is such a dying death? Shall he be hid
Within a darksome grave, who thus ascends,
A god, to enter heaven's open gates?

No. Mozart lives! Soon will he come before you!
Then cleanse your hearts; shut every sense
Close 'gainst the din of commonplace pursuits,
And fit yourselves to hear the Master's tones,
Which, like a benediction, soon shall fall
Upon all here! And when your hearts are full,
Then spread abroad 'mongst all of German birth,
The master's fame! He who could thus create!
The people's fame from whose strong loins he sprung,
The city's fame that boasts of such a son!

II

THE COMPOSER'S DOMESTIC LIFE

AMONGST the thousands that came together to do honor to the composer's memory there was neither man, woman nor child who could boast that Mozart's blood, though never so diluted, flowed in his or her veins. Not a single descendant of Mozart is alive to-day. In 1842 when the statue, modelled by Schwanthaler, was unveiled in the Mozartplatz, two of the composer's sons, all of his children that had outlived infancy, were still living. One of them, the younger, who received his father's name, Wolfgang Amadeus, and adopted his father's profession, attended the unveiling ceremonies, and was appointed Honorary Chapelmaster to the Dom Musikverein and the Mozarteum. Two years later he died at Karlsbad at the age of fifty-three. He was less than six months old when his illustrious father died, and though it is said that some of the latter's physical, mental and moral traits were pre-

HIS DOMESTIC LIFE

served in him, he inherited nothing of his genius. He was a respectable musician, that is all. His elder brother, Carl, born in Vienna in 1783, lived until 1858, for years filling the function of a modest Austrian official, a book-keeper of some kind, I think, and died in Milan. Neither of the two married, and with Carl the name of Mozart died. Within the nine years of Mozart's married life (1782-1791) six children, four sons and two daughters, were born to him. Carl, who lived longest and latest, was the first born; the musical son, Wolfgang, was the last. In the museum housed in the building No. 9 Getreidegasse, third floor, where the composer was born, there is a counterfeit presentment of the two, which was painted by a Danish artist, and was once the property of Mozart's widow, who bequeathed it to her sister, describing it in her will as a "painting of fraternal affection." Mozart left Salzburg just before the birth of his first son, and never saw the city after 1783.

The Augsburg family of Mozart (or "Motzert," as it seems from recent discoveries they were called in the seventeenth century) died out long before the Salzburg family. Of the latter the only descendants are in the female line. Wolfgang's sister, Marie Anna, or Marianne, (the "Nannerl" of his childhood's letters,) married in 1784 while her father was yet alive. She had a son who became a Mauthhauscontroleur (tax official), and died in Bregenz leaving a daughter, the only grandniece of the composer. This daughter became the wife of a military official in Innsbruck, who afterward changed his habitation to Graz, where she gave birth to a son who, when last I heard of him, was a lieutenant in a Hanoverian regiment. His name is Gustav Forster, and he is presumably the last of the female line of Mozarts. His whereabouts was not known to the committee, and he was not invited to the festival. An aged widow, the Baroness von Sonnenburg, who bears some relation, probably by marriage, with the family into which Marie Anna married, was living in 1891 in a retreat for women kept by some nuns near Salzburg. She was invited to attend the festival but returned the tickets on the ground of her great age and infirmity. Mozart's widow married the Danish Councillor Nissen, author of a biography of the composer, in 1809, and lived till 1820 in Copenhagen. In that year she returned to Salzburg, and died in March, 1842, just as the model of Schwanthaler's statue reached the city.

The musical Bachs lived through so many generations that their family name became a generic one for the town-musicians in Thuringia. The musical Beethovens numbered several generations before their culmination in the master to whom Mozart surrendered his sceptre. The strong root, the perfect flower and fruit, the withered tree of the musical Mozarts were all compassed by a century and a quarter. The year 1719 saw the birth of Leopold, the year 1844 the death of his grandson, Wolfgang Amadeus.

There was no grave to deck with flowers. Mozart's body was lowered into a pauper's grave, and not a single loving eye took note of the spot. The widow was ill and did not attend the burial. A few friends who went as far as the church when the last words were said were deterred from going farther by a storm of rain and snow. For months the widow seemed indifferent as to the disposition of the mortal remains of her husband, whose genius she never half appreciated, and when tardy inquiries were made it was impossible to learn where the grave had been dug. The case seems incomprehensible, but by a strange coincidence it was repeated forty-eight years later in New-York, when Da Ponte, the librettist of "Don Giovanni," "Le Nozze di Figaro" and "Cosi fan tutte," was buried. In some respects the mystery of the poet's burial was even stranger than that of the composer. Mozart died neglected by his friends and was buried as a pauper; Da Ponte was surrounded by rich and influential friends to the last, and some of the most eminent men in New-York City followed his body in procession to the grave. The Italian societies of the city started a movement to erect a monument to his memory, yet when, in 1887, I made a most diligent and painstaking search I could not find a trace of his burial place, and it was only with difficulty that the fact could be established that the interment had taken place in the old Eleventh-Street Cemetery. More than this, even the official record of his death is wrong in the city's books.

There is a tradition, which seems well supported, that Mozart's widow and her second husband, with whom she lived in such comfort and contentment as she never knew during her first marriage, were interred in the grave first occupied by the composer's father. It is in the Sebastian Kirchhof in Salzburg.

HIS DOMESTIC LIFE

Madame Nissen, she who had been Constanze Mozart, *née* Weber (she was own cousin to the composer of "Der Freischütz"), outlived her second husband sixteen years and though she had not taken the trouble to note the location of Mozart's grave she provided Nissen with a tombstone and an epitaph which celebrated all his virtues and worldly achievements and wound up with a pitiful example of mortuary verse. Thirty years ago the old grave-digger who had buried the pair used to tell visitors that the grave in which Nissen was first laid and then his widow had been that of the composer's father. Of that fact Constanze left no sign. Plainly the tender care which she received from the petty Danish Councillor weaned her from whatever love she had left for the Mozarts.

More than all else that is known of the composer, the circumstances of his burial testify to the struggle against poverty which the most generously gifted musician that ever lived had to fight. Most mournfully do they also tell of the hollowness of the affection of those who called themselves his friends (I fear also of the indifference of his wife), of the depravity of the social instincts, as well as the artistic appreciation of the

Viennese public of a century ago. Why the simple beauty of Mozart's music should have strained the capacity of the Viennese a little more than a hundred years ago, it is difficult to understand, but nothing is truer than that in his lifetime the unique position that he now occupies in our appreciation was never given to Mozart. His popularity never reached that of Salieri, for instance, whose operas triumphed over Mozart's as easily as a quarter of a century later Rossini's measures prevented appreciation of Beethoven's. This was true not only in Vienna, but throughout Germany. It was with no little astonishment that I took note, while investigating the records of the Grand Ducal Theatre at Weimar during Goethe's artistic administration, of the fact that Mozart's operas were outnumbered in performance many times by the works of pigmies whose names are now forgotten, to say nothing of composers like Weigl, Salieri and Dittersdorf. In spite of its production of geniuses, it was a frivolous period in art. In opera the era of extravagant spectacle was just past, and the dramatic spirit begotten by Gluck and Mozart was yet in its swaddling clothes. The vocal virtuoso was still dominant.

The relics of the Mozart family preserved

HIS DOMESTIC LIFE

in Salzburg do not help a visitor to realize the fact that Mozart lived in poverty. One reason of this is that outside of the manuscripts (autograph letters and compositions) the majority of them either date back to his childhood or came from well-to-do sources. It might serve a purpose if the official inventory of his possessions taken after his death were obtained from the archives at Vienna and displayed in the room where he was born. Even Otto Jahn neglected to reprint this pitifully eloquent document in his exhaustive biography. Its items deserve to be made public; they are as follows: Cash, sixty florins; arrears of salary (eight hundred florins a year), one hundred and thirty-three florins, twenty kreutzers; credits (appraised as worthless), eight hundred florins; three silver tablespoons valued at seven florins; clothing and linen, forty-nine florins; table linen, seventeen florins; furniture in the first room, twenty-one florins; in the second, eighty-two florins, thirty kreutzers; in the third, sixty-four florins; the principal item being a billiard table valued at sixty florins; in the fourth, one hundred and eighty-nine florins, the principal item here being a pianoforte, "with pedal," valued at eighty florins; library, seventy florins.

Estimating the florin at its present value in American money the property which Mozart left at his death was worth less than three hundred dollars.

The two rooms in which Leopold Mozart lived in the Getreidegasse, in one of which the composer was born in 1756, are modest enough in good sooth, but they do not differ from those in which the majority of Salzburg's citizens live to-day. The house itself is of the architectural style and degree of comfort, or want of comfort, found in hundreds of its fellows. It partakes of the essential characteristics of Salzburg, which are closeness and gloominess. The low stairway by which one ascends to the third floor is of stone and vaulted. As life was in Salzburg one hundred years ago, as life is in Salzburg to-day, a poet might occupy the rooms. So might a shoemaker. I dare say the juxtaposition of poet and shoemaker might be found in the town now. The family portraits in oil on the walls, though of no value as works of art, give the impression that the Mozarts were in comfortable circumstances.

To those unfamiliar with the keyed instruments of his day, the composer's clavichord and pianoforte, which are on exhibition,

HIS DOMESTIC LIFE

teach a useful object lesson. Very wisely, they are kept strung up and tuned, and there is no prohibition against touching them. Many times in the course of festival week strains from Mozart's compositions came tinkling from the corner opposite to that in which little Woferl's cradle stood. The smaller instrument is generally called a spinet in the books, but this is an error; it is a clavichord, the strings being struck by a bit of brass on the end of each key, not plucked by a quill as in the case of the spinet. The thriftiness of the times is suggested by the sight of a package of "The Genuine Court Plaister, London," which a memorandum, supposed to be in the handwriting of Nissen, says was brought by Mozart from London. On his visit to the English metropolis he was seven years old. Evidently Woferl was not permitted to play with a penknife; otherwise a single package of court plaster would not have lasted him throughout his boyhood and a score of years beyond.

The other spots in Salzburg with which the name of Mozart is associated invite reflections concerning the social and artistic life of the period in which he lived chiefly. Personal memories, poetical though not altogether savory, in spite of the efforts of his biographer to purge his private character, cling around the little house on a slope of the Capuzinerberg which was brought from Vienna and in which in the summer of 1791 Mozart completed his "Zauberflöte." The tales of the life which Mozart led with roystering companions of both sexes in this tiny box of a house (it consists of but one room and is not more than twenty feet long and fifteen wide) are discredited now, but it is not impossible that they account, to some extent, for the unfeeling conduct of Constanze, the widow, touching his grave. To attribute his death to dissipations indulged in during the last summer of his life is probably as foolish a performance as the latter day effort to present him as a model of conjugal fidelity and affection. The "Zauberflötehäuschen," as it is called, is now a museum of portraits and commemorative wreaths. The cathedral in which some of the precocious boy's religious music was first heard, is a magnificent edifice which, when contrasted in company with the Archiepiscopal palaces and gardens, with the absurdly small and wretched theatre, speaks volumes concerning the attitude of the Prince-Archbishops of Salzburg toward art.

HIS DOMESTIC LIFE

Opposite the theatre, in what is now called the Markartplatz, is another house, which was occupied by the family of Leopold as a dwelling, from which Wolfgang departed when he left the service of the Prince-Archbishop and betook himself to Vienna. Like the birth-house it is disfigured by a sign reaching entirely across the front announcing the fact that it is "Mozart's Wohnhaus." A tasteful tablet, it seems, would not have proclaimed the pride which Salzburg feels at having given birth to such a son with sufficient emphasis. It took gilded letters a foot and a half high to do that.

Travellers know the marvellous natural beauty of Salzburg's position in the valley of the Salzach — how snugly a portion of it nestles under the cliffs of the Mönchsberg on the left bank of the river, hugging the sheer rock so closely that it actually overhangs the houses in one of the streets and how, where the valley widens toward Hohensalzburg, crowned by the castle-fortress, it opens out in the squares, each with its quaint fountain or statue, that afford approaches to the few large structures in the city. Except on the opposite bank of the river, where the graceful slopes of the Capuzinerberg give easy foothold to lovely villas that smile from out the deep foliage of gardens and forests, and the wider plain left by the retreat of the mountains from the river is filled by buildings of a modern type, the idea of spaciousness is utterly foreign to the town. The streets are narrow and wind about in the most bewildering manner, following in a general but devious way the course of the river. Cross streets are few; in fact, glancing along the house-fronts one might easily fancy that the need of going across-town had never occurred to the builders. Instead of cross streets there are hundreds of arched courts which afford passage from one winding street to another. The general effect, enhanced by the narrowness of the streets, is one of prison-like gloominess, and only the bright sunlight of festival week and the banners which hung from the majority of the houses gave the city a cheery appearance. No vista being more than one or two hundred feet long, a few bits of bunting had great decorative potency. The Mozartplatz was quite gayly caparisoned, flowering plants being banked around the base of the Mozart statue, and rows of festooned standards bounding the entire square. The torchlight procession of the first night and garden fête of the second were marred

HIS DOMESTIC LIFE

by rain, but the enthusiasm of the participants in the former was proof against the wet. The line of march was not curtailed a foot, the procession numbered thousands, including some of the artists of the festival. As each division reached the Mozart monument a large wreath of laurel was deposited beside the pedestal. Finally the united singers of the town, who had already halted and sung in front of the birth-house, raised the strains of Mozart's "Bundeslied," after which the torches (which were immense candles instead of oil lamps) were extinguished. The most costly feature of the celebration was the garden fête in the Mirabellgarten. On the attendance here the financial outcome of the festival depended. Rain came rather early in the evening, but the old palace grounds were already crowded at fifty kreutzers a head, and the committee were saved. There was a deficit, but it was trifling.

III

MUSIC AT THE FESTIVAL

As may have already been surmised, there was a great contrast between the musical features of the centennial celebration of Mozart's death and the festival's external conditions and circumstances. This contrast, however, was a generous contributor to the amiability which characterized the occasion. In it was reflected some of the geniality and the simplicity of the great composer's nature. Though ten thousand persons listened, lovingly and reverentially, to the "Requiem" in the cathedral, only about four hundred and fifty were privileged to attend the festival representation of "The Marriage of Figaro," which brought the celebration to a close. The four hundred and fifty enjoyed a rare sensation, to which sentiment contributed quite as much as the performance; the excluded thousands accepted the situation with charming good humor. Between the mass, which opened the festival, and the opera, which brought it to a close, were two concerts by the Philharmonic Society of Vienna, under the direction of Wilhelm Jahn, director of the Imperial Court Opera. These concerts took place in the Aula Academica, a plain, old-fashioned hall, in which candles are still depended on for light when the room is used at night. Here again the seating accommodations, though three times as great as those of the theatre, were inadequate. Yet the good humor of the visitors suffered no impairment.

The environment was provincial, the concerts metropolitan. Much of the music dated from the last year of Mozart's life. The "Requiem" was the last composition in his thoughts; he did not live to finish it. The symphonies played were those in G minor and C major ("Jupiter"), both written in the summer of 1788. The "Bundeslied," sung before the monument on the conclusion of the torchlight procession, dates from his death-year. The opera "Le Nozze di Figaro" was produced five years before his death. Its choice for representation was doubtless due to the fact that the stage of the theatre is too small to permit the mounting of "Die Zauberflöte," obviously the right choice for the festival as a product of the composer's last year. "Don Giovanni" was first announced by the committee, but the opera based on Beaumarchais's comedy was substituted for it, probably because the centenary of Mozart's masterpiece had been celebrated in 1887. The circumstance that the occasion was also a centennial anniversary of the composition of "Die Zauberflöte" was also remembered in the compilation of the programme of the first concert in the Aula Academica on July 16, at 11 A. M., one-third of which was devoted to excerpts from the work, which, according to the dictum of Beethoven, is to be set down as the first essentially German opera.

The forces employed in the performance of the "Requiem" were a chorus selected from the cathedral choir, the women's choir of the Mozarteum, and the men's singing societies of Salzburg; the orchestras of the Dom Musikverein and the Mozarteum; Mesdames E. Brandt-Forster, and Louise Kaulich and Messieurs Gustave Walter and Franz von Reichenberg, of the Court Opera at Vienna. J. F. Hummel, director of the Mozarteum, conducted the performance. The choir numbered two hundred voices and was an admirable body whose singing reflected greater credit on the city than the orchestral accompaniment, which, though satisfactory, was not remarkable. The inadequacy of the instrumental part of the performance was explained by Director Hummel on the ground of a restriction in number compelled by the dimensions of the choir-loft. He had to choose between a large choir with small orchestra and a large orchestra with small choir. Arguing correctly enough that the "Requiem" was essentially a choral composition, he chose the former. Instrumental music is cultivated with great assiduity and earnestness in the conservatory connected with the Mozarteum, Director Hummel compelling every free student of the pianoforte or violin to take up a wind instrument in addition, and I could easily believe him when he said that it was not a want of orchestral players but a want of room in the gallery which invited to the only criticism that was passed upon the artistic side of the performance.

For the first concert in the Aula this was the programme:

Excerpts from "Die Zauberflöte."
(a) Overture.
(b) Duet, "Bei Männern welche Liebe fühlen."
    (Mme. E. Brandt-Forster and Josef Ritter.)

A MOZART CENTENARY

(c) Air: "In diesen heil'gen Hallen." (Franz von Reichenberg.)

(d) Air: "Dies Bildniss ist bezaubernd schön." (Gustav Walter.)

(e) *Pamina's* grand air. (Mme. Brandt-Forster.)

(f) Air and chorus: "O Isis und Osiris." (Franz von Reichenberg and Salzburger Liedertafel.)

Concerto for Pianoforte in D minor. (Madame Essipoff-Leschetizky.)

Symphony in G minor.

The programme of the second concert at the same hour on the third day of the festival, July 17, was this:

String quartet, D minor. (The Hellmesberger Quartet, of Vienna.)

Air from "Cosi fan tutte." (Gustav Walter.)

Adagio from the quintet in G minor. (String orchestra.)

Air from "Die Entführung aus dem Serail." (Mme. Marie Wilt.)

Songs: "Das Veilchen," "Vergiss Mein Nicht" and "Wiegenlied." (Fraulein Frederike Mayer.)

"Jupiter" Symphony.

It has been said that Mozart's music can only be heard in its perfection in Vienna. I do not know how this may be; I have heard many poor Mozart singers who hailed from the Austro-Hungarian Court Opera, but I am willing to believe that those who live in the social and artistic atmosphere of Vienna for a time may acquire a sympathetic appreciation for the spirit of Mozart which the people of a colder and more phlegmatic north will never imbibe. The dividing line between musical creation and recreation is exceedingly fine — that fact it is which makes it possible for an executive musician to become entitled to the name of artist — and unless an interpreter can feel with some of its original potency the influence that impelled the composer, his interpretation will speak a different dialect, if not a different tongue, from that native to the composition. I would rather find an explanation of the beauty of the Philharmonic Society's performance of the two symphonies in this relationship between the composer and his interpreters, difficult as it may be to analyze, than to rest on that weak reed commonly spoken of as tradition. Musical tradition is a very uncertain quantity. The Bayreuth festivals have failed to preserve Wagner's manner, though established and maintained for that very purpose. Yet the Bayreuth festivals are only twenty-two years old, and Wagner has been dead less than two decades. Nevertheless, the strongest wish that I felt while listening to the two symphonies on this occasion was to believe that it was thus that they sounded in the inspired fancy of their creator. Of the weak sentimentality with which so many conductors infuse Mozart's music there was not a trace in Herr Jahn's interpretation. All was splendidly sane and joyously vigorous. The muscularity of the band's string-tone and its ebullient vivacity in the minuet of the G-minor Symphony made the music as sonorous as that of an ultra modern composer utilizing the large and varied apparatus of to-day.

The spirit thus manifested is beyond question inherent in Mozart's great works. It is the element that has preserved them while those of his contemporaries have perished. So far as it is permitted us to speak of immortality in connection with a musical composition (of all art works the most perishable by reason of its nature), it is this spirit which made Mozart's chief works immortal. They can ever be read so as to interpret the feelings of the readers. The thought is not confined by its formal investiture. Yet while Herr Jahn read the symphonies in this vital manner, he did not

MUSIC AT THE FESTIVAL

in any way distort them. Their utterance remained simple and ingenuous. It was particularly gratifying to find him untouched by the desire to win interest for the music by the pedantic devices with which some conductors are now seeking to make plain the purposes of composers, as they say. He did not distort the minuet of the "Jupiter" symphony by playing it so slowly as to rob the melody of its native character. This is a part of the mischief that has resulted from Wagner's criticism of the tempo in which Mendelssohn and other conductors were in the habit of playing the corresponding movement in Beethoven's eighth symphony. That criticism has given birth to the notion that a symphonic minuet must be played in the tempo of the old dance for which Mozart set a standard in the minuet to which his nobility step it so decorously in the first finale of "Don Giovanni," — a notion which never occurred to either Haydn, Mozart or Beethoven, as should be obvious enough from the character inherent in the themes of their symphonic minuets. In a less degree, but still very noticeably, the same fresh and vigorous style of reading marked Madame Essipoff's playing in the concerto — especially at the rehearsal which had been thrown open to the public at the price of a gulden, in order to accommodate the many who could not obtain tickets to the concert.

The festival performance of Mozart's comic opera, which concluded the centennial celebration, took place in the Royal Imperial Theatre. Between the magnificence of this title and the dimensions and appearance of the playhouse there is a discrepancy which was well calculated to heighten the careless gayety of the festive solemnity. The theatre dates back to the period of Mozart's slavery under the Prince-Archbishop Hieronymus Colloredo. Previous to 1775 it was a *Ballhaus*. In that year it was transformed into a theatre. After my experience I am inclined to believe that in that year, too, it was hermetically sealed, in order to preserve the atmosphere sanctified by the exhalations from the archiepiscopal body of the pious Hieronymus. Mozart was then nineteen years old, and for two years longer he remained in the service of the Prince-Archbishop as concert-meister of the Hofcapelle without salary. His youthful operas had been written for other cities, not for Salzburg, whose ruler was indisposed to give commissions, which might have cost a little money, to the genius that was giving the city renown; but as the Mozart family, who lived directly opposite the theatre, across what is now called the Markartplatz, were industrious theatre-goers, it is unquestioned that Wolfgang was a frequent visitor at the theatre, and doubtless a frequent performer at entertainments there. It is probable, therefore, that when I stood within those *heil'gen Hallen* and inhaled the carefully conserved atmosphere of a century ago, I breathed the air which Mozart had breathed. Strangely enough, I did not like it. The idiosyncratic desire of a nineteenth century American for fresh air was stronger than my reverence for this Mozartian relic, but it availed naught against the strong repugnance which Germans and Austrians feel within doors for the elixir which they cannot do without when they are eating or drinking. Out of doors the air was as balmy as a sleeping baby's breath. Had it been stirred into a tornado and sent down the backbone of every German in the place, with his chronic susceptibility to taking a cold increased a thousandfold by the internal warmth of festal enthusiasm, it could not have produced a single sneeze. Yet a piteously gentle plea that the door, behind the heavy curtains (so

A MOZART CENTENARY

hung as to intercept the cupful of air which might surreptitiously steal into the audience-room with a late-comer), might be left ajar a few inches for a moment between the acts, called out a look of horror on a score of faces and an awestricken protestation that a draught would result which plainly all believed would be deadlier than miners' damp. So the half dozen Americans in the audience sweltered and stewed patiently for four hours in the nauseous atmosphere of the playhouse and tried to forget the approaching headache in the enjoyment of Mozart's music.

This Royal Imperial Theatre has the dimensions of such a suite of rooms as a thrifty newspaper reporter can hire in New York. By placing benches in the parquet instead of chairs to save the space wasted in ordinary playhouses by the chair-arms, it is made to accommodate three hundred and fifty human beings of average breadth and thickness. Several more could find room were it not that at the end opposite the stage there is a Royal Imperial box, which, I fancy, was once the Prince-Archiepiscopal box. Upon its tawdry upholstery and hangings, I doubt not, the eyes of Mozart, only twenty-one years old when he emancipated himself from the slavery in which his spiritual and temporal lord held him, often fell. On this occasion these relics of a former tuppenny magnificence surrounded an Austrian Archduke, who looked through his opera glasses at a few young women whom he might almost have touched without leaving his seat and then lost interest in the entertainment. By opening the gallery and issuing eighty tickets for standing places, the committee raised the capacity of the house for this festival representation to about five hundred. What the percentage of deaths from asphyxiation may have been in the gallery I do not know. Not hearing of any deaths I took it for granted that there were no Americans there. The proscenium opening may have been twenty feet broad (I am disposed to be liberal in such estimates) and the same number of feet deep. If it was necessary to use the theatre these dimensions will suggest an explanation of the conduct of the Festival Committee in celebrating the hundredth anniversary of the composition of "The Magic Flute" (for the centenary of that opera and the "Requiem" as well as Mozart's death was commemorated in the festival) in relegating the music of Mozart's mystical phantasmagoria and singular fairytale to the concert-room. Yet it was in this

A MOZART CENTENARY

same theatre that the centennial representation of "Don Giovanni" took place in 1887 when artists like Bianchi, Marie Lehmann (sister of the greater Lilli), Reichmann, Staudigl and Marie Wilt sang and Hans Richter wielded the baton. With the actors' "cabin'd, cribb'd, confined," by the stage the finale of the first act of Mozart's masterpiece must have looked comical enough. In "Le Nozze," Frau Ende-Andriessen, of the Municipal Opera at Cologne, sang the part of the *Countess*. In respect of both latitude and longitude she meets the most extravagant demands of Wagner's Norse heroines, and when she "took" the stage she literally left very little of it for the other personages. Her presence in the final garden scene simplified the work of concealment which makes up so much of the "business" of the act.

The characters in the opera were in the hands of the following artists: *Count Almaviva*, Josef Ritter, of Hamburg and Vienna; *The Countess*, Frau Ende-Andriessen, of Cologne; *Susanne*, Fräulein Bianca Bianchi, of Buda-Pesth; *Cherubino*, Frau Brandt-Forster, of the Court Opera at Vienna; *Figaro*, Herr Franz Krolop, of the Court Opera at Berlin; *Marcellina*, Frau Louise Kaulich, of the Court Opera at Vienna;

MUSIC AT THE FESTIVAL

Dr. Bartolo, Herr Rudolf Freny, of the Municipal Opera at Hamburg; *Don Basilio*, Herr Victor Schmidt, of the Court Opera at Vienna; *Guzman*, Herr Anton Schnittenhelm, of the Court Opera at Vienna; *Barbara*, Fräulein Anna Hauser, of the Court Opera at Vienna; *Antonio*, Herr Benedikt Felix, Court Opera at Vienna. The conductor was Director J. F. Hummel, of the Mozarteum, and the orchestra, of necessity small, but still efficient, was a local body.

Whether or not German singers can do justice to Mozart has always been a question in my mind. I am not insensible to the fact that in all of the genial master's works there is a something in which the sincerity of German feeling is manifest, and that it is largely this feeling which supplies the element that has preserved his operas while those of his rivals have been forgotten. In "The Marriage of Figaro" there is little playroom for honest sentiment, and Mozart's music is as lighthearted and careless as the play. It is musical champagne from beginning to end, varied by a single draught of still wine at the beginning of the second act (*Porge amor*) — and that an Italian sweet wine rather than a fragrant Hock. In "Don Giovanni," the tragic spirit with which

Mozart infused the play in spite of Da Ponte's purpose that the buffo element should always be in the foreground, gives German interpreters an opportunity to exploit the side of their artistic nature which is essentially native to them and in which they excel. They have felt with Mozart, while Italian singers have felt with his librettist. The fate of *Don Juan* has in it a tragic awfulness which casts its shadow before for those of German feeling; for the Italian stage artist it is only a conclusion to the play which enables *Leporello*, in hiding under the table, to amuse the spectators by an exhibition of clownish fear. Musical comedy of the Italian type, whose loftiest examples are the *Figaro* operas of Mozart and Rossini, demands some things which seem almost impossible to German singers. Even when they use the Italian language they generally fall short of perfection, because of a want of that nimbleness of tongue which is easy to the Latin. When an opera composed to Italian words is sung in German the retention of all of its comic spirit is simply impossible. The volatile utterance which is so essential an element in music of this character and of which there are many examples in "Figaro's Marriage," is utterly

MUSIC AT THE FESTIVAL

foreign to the German tongue. A German *Dr. Bartolo* is inconceivable. Even if the translator should show due regard for the bits of characterization in which the buffo music of Mozart and Rossini abounds, and should have the most perfect command of his language, he would inevitably make shipwreck in scores of places on the consonantal rocks which are strewed all over the German lingual ocean.

The finale of the second act of "The Marriage of Figaro" is a model of ensemble writing which has never had a fellow. In it the music and action run riot and a race from beginning to end, each accentuating the points made by the other, neither ever hindering, but both working together toward a dramatic climax which is irresistible in its effect. At this festival performance, the finale was sung with vastly more vivacity than I expected to find, the singers bringing into the performance some of the gayety and lightness of temperament belonging to the Austrian capital, but there could be no escape from the fetters of language. The air was thick with sluggish consonants and lingering sibilants. This lingual clog retarded the merry flood of music throughout and compelled the judicious to take refuge in a standard of judgment recognizing the insurmountable difficulties of the German book. From this new view-point there was much to admire in the performance, though the voices of the singers were deadened, deprived of all resonance, by the stagnant atmosphere of the theatre. The honors were easily borne off by Frau Brandt-Forster, in the rôle of the *Page*, but as to what proportion of her success was due to her lovely face and arch acting and what to her voice and singing I shall not express an opinion. Brandt-Forster was popular in Vienna. Artistically, I was told, she had not met the expectations of Director Jahn, who on the expiration of her first engagement manifested a desire to let her seek employment elsewhere. But the University students were enamoured of her pretty face, and a round-robin, signed by about three hundred of them, brought Herr Jahn to terms. Which incident might furnish a text for a sermon on the influences which sway the high priests in our art-temples, in Europe as elsewhere, if I were disposed to preach. But I am not.

IV

DA PONTE IN NEW YORK

It was a sincere cause of regret in the fall of 1887, when the principal cities of Europe celebrated the hundredth anniversary of the first performance of " Don Giovanni," that the season of opera at the Metropolitan Opera House was not yet begun. Otherwise New York would also have joined in the celebration, in which it had a unique interest, from the fact that it was the home for more than a quarter of a century of the poet who wrote the book of Mozart's masterpiece. At the commemoration by the Grand Opera of Paris the original manuscript score of the opera, which is owned by Madame Viardot-Garcia (daughter of the first representative of *Don Giovanni* in the United States), was exhibited to the public in the foyer of the Opera House. In Dresden the Tonkünstler-Verein, hearing that Luigi Bassi, who "created" the rôle of the dissolute *Don* at the first representation, lay buried in a Dresden cemetery, caused the singer's long neglected grave to be restored and a marble cross, bearing a suitable inscription, to be placed over it.

Thus was a simple singer honored, while the resting places of the colossal genius who created the music, and the gifted and ingenious poet who provided him with the poetry to which he might wed that music, must remain without a distinguishing mark. Mozart's dust lies in a pauper's grave in Vienna; but where, no one knows. The grave was never marked; the plot in which it was made was one that was dug up every ten years and filled anew. A storm drove back the friends who started out to attend the burial, and no one saw the body lowered except the sexton and his assistants. A noble friend, who had undertaken the care of the funeral because of the illness of Mozart's widow, and who had expended eleven florins and thirty-six kreutzers on it (say about five dollars), did not inquire where the body had been put, and when the widow visited the churchyard, after her recovery, the gravediggers had been changed and no one knew where the remains of the great musician lay.

That was in December, 1791, in Vienna. Almost half a century later Lorenzo Da Ponte, the Italian poet who had been

DA PONTE IN NEW YORK

Mozart's friend and collaborator with him on three operas, "Le Nozze di Figaro," "Don Giovanni," and "Cosi fan Tutte," died in New York. He had lived in the New World a full generation, — more than one-third of a marvellously checkered life, the term of which embraced the birth and death of Mozart, Beethoven, Schubert, Byron, Scott, and Napoleon Bonaparte, and the entire creative career of Haydn; he had been *improvvisatore*, professor of rhetoric, and politician in his native land; poet to the Imperial Theatre and Latin secretary to the Emperor in Austria;[1] Italian teacher, operatic poet, littérateur, and bookseller in England; tradesman, teacher, opera manager, and bookseller in America. He had enjoyed the friendship of some of the great ones of the Old World, and some of the noble ones of the New, and in New York he came nearer to finding a home than anywhere in Europe. He died within the recollection of

---

[1] Da Ponte sometimes spoke of himself as "Poet to the Emperor Joseph II." His biographers have almost unanimously accepted the statement that he was what these words indicate, a poet laureate, or "Poeta Cesario," of Austria. Such is not the case. In a foot-note in the appendix to the third volume, last edition of his "Memorie," he corrects the error, saying that he never was Cæsarian poet, but that his title was "Poet to the Imperial theatres."

many persons yet alive, and men whose names shine brightly in local annals followed him to his grave; yet the exact location of that grave is unknown. In August, 1887, I made a laborious search for it. All available records pointed to the old Roman Catholic cemetery in Eleventh-street, between Avenue A and First-avenue, as the graveyard that had received the body of the distinguished nonagenarian just forty-nine years before. The place is overgrown with rank grass and weeds. There are no paths. Those who wish to read the inscriptions on the headstones must stumble along as best they can; now over irregular hillocks, now into deep depressions half-filled with old boots, rusty tin cans, and other refuse. Many of the inscriptions have been obliterated by the action of the elements; some of the stones lie prone upon the ground (the bones which once they guarded having been removed, as the bright-eyed, fresh-faced, silver-haired old wife of the decrepit keeper explains), and in one place a large Ailantus tree in growing has taken up a stone half-way into itself. For hours I crossed and recrossed the decaying cemetery, scrutinizing carefully every inscription; but in vain. No head-stone was found bearing the name of Da Ponte, and there are no records to identify the spot where, on August 20, 1838, his grave was dug.

The life of Lorenzo Da Ponte has not often been told; it has never been all told, and the narratives which have found their way into print are full of inaccuracies. In Oulibischeff's book on Mozart his death is said to have occurred in December, 1838, instead of August, and when the municipality of his native town, about a generation ago, wanted to erect a monument to him, it was found necessary to apply to New York to learn the date of his death. If at that time an answer was returned by the municipality of New York, and the official records were consulted for the information, the chances are that an incorrect date was sent to Ceneda, for the records of the Health Department assert that Lorenzo Daponte (thus the name is written)[1] died on August 21, 1838, which was four days after the true date and one day after his burial. The books are equally contradictory as to the date of his arrival in America, and many other incidents in his career. Many of

[1] It is curious that in Longworth's New York Directory Da Ponte's name was written with two capital letters until 1821, and that thenceforward it remained " Daponte " until his death. Tuckerman also calls him " Daponte." The French translator of the " Memorie," with obvious stupidity, calls him " d'Aponte."

these contradictions are doubtless due to the want of definiteness which characterizes the Italian autobiography which Da Ponte published in New York seventy-five years ago. In this work, which has been translated into German and French, but not into English, Da Ponte is garrulous enough about many insignificant things, but silent about many others of vastly more importance, and his biographers in the hand-books on music and literature have pretty generally evinced an unwillingness to be guided in all things by Da Ponte's own utterances. My inquiry, which occupied several weeks, discovered many interesting things touching the American career of Da Ponte, some having almost a serio-comic aspect.

Lorenzo Da Ponte was an assumed name. The real name of him who made it celebrated is unknown. He was the son of a Hebrew leather dealer in Ceneda, a small town of the Venetian republic. Until his fourteenth year he was brought up a Jew, but having attracted the attention of the Roman Catholic bishop of Ceneda, Lorenzo Da Ponte, by his precocious talents, the latter gave him an education and his name.[1] After five years of

---

[1] Whether Da Ponte ever took orders or was only a self-styled Abbé is not clear. In a scurrilous Italian

DA PONTE IN NEW YORK

study he went to Venice, whence amorous escapades compelled him to flee to Treviso. There he became professor of rhetoric, and candidate for office, lampooned his opponent in a sonnet, and was ordered to leave the republic of Venice. He went to Dresden, then to Vienna, where Salieri aided him and he received from Joseph II the position of Poet to the Imperial Theatre and Latin Secretary. There, too, he fell in with Mozart, who asked him to throw Beaumarchais's comedy, " Le Mariage de Figaro," into an opera. The collaboration was the first happy one that Mozart had had, and the opera was a tremendous success, especially in Prague. Mozart promised to write another opera for the people who understood him so well, and this time Da Ponte suggested "Don Giovanni." To Da Ponte, therefore, belongs the credit of having suggested the

pamphlet directed against him, printed in Lisbon, there is a sonnet inscribed "to the ineffable merit of the Jew, Lorenzo Daponte, poet of the Italian theatre in London, who, after having been converted to Christianity in the city of Venice, embraced the churchly state so successfully that he reached the dignity of a priest; but come to England, would wear no other robe than that of an impostor, and kicked aside the 'Dominus vobiscum,' in order to increase the number of rascals." A reply to this pamphlet, which, it may be safely assumed, came from Da Ponte, attributes the authorship to one Carlo Francesco.

story and written the book of this masterpiece, whose chances of immortality are surely as great as those of any other musical composition. Da Ponte won the ill will of Leopold, and when Joseph II died he had to leave Vienna. Meanwhile he had married an English woman at Trieste, whither he went to seek a reconciliation with Leopold. Armed with a letter to Marie Antoinette, who had admired some of his works, he started for Paris, but when he got to Spires " it was in the hands of the French and Antoinette was a prisoner in the temple." He changed his plans and went to London, where a year later he became poet to the Italian Opera and aided Taylor in the management. He also started a bookstore and went into the printing business. The latter venture and his indorsement of Taylor's bills involved him financially, and fleeing from the officers of the law he came to America.

It is at this point that my investigations began, and their first result was to establish the date of Da Ponte's arrival in America. Grove's "Dictionary of Music and Musicians" says that he sailed from England March 5, 1803; H. T. Tuckerman wrote in an article in "Putnam's Magazine" that he arrived at Philadelphia on June 4, 1802; F.

DA PONTE IN NEW YORK

L. Ritter lands him in May, 1803. All agree that his financial troubles drove him from England. Now for the new evidence. In the library of the New York Historical Society there is a copy of a pamphlet which hitherto has remained unmentioned by all who have written on Da Ponte so far as can be learned. It was his first public utterance in America, and was evidently designed as the first of a series of publications to be circulated among his Italian scholars in this city. It is in Italian, with an English translation, and the copy in question was uncut until it fell into the writer's hands. Here is the title in English:

Compendium of the Life of Lorenzo Da Ponte, written by Himself, to which is added the first Literary Conversazione held at His House in New York on the 10th day of March, 1807, consisting of several Italian compositions in verse and prose, translated into English by his scholars. New York, printed by I. Riley & Co., 1807.

Da Ponte's motive for printing this pamphlet is told in the brief prefatory address "To the Reader," as follows:

It is now a long while since I promised to my friends the story of my life. I will shortly fulfil my promise. Certain reasons have, however, induced me to publish, for the present, these few hints. If they ever reach England I hope those persons may read them who are unjustly taking advantage of my absence to deprive me even of that little which has escaped the hands of fraud; and which I entrusted before my departure to apparent honesty. I wish to conceal their names under the veil of charity, if I can no longer under that of friendship; and, if they be willing, it is not too late.

In this "Compendium" Da Ponte hurries over the greater portion of his life-history. His departure from Venice, he chronicles thus: "I was obliged to leave Venice, the place of my nativity, for having associated myself with an illustrious person whose efforts were directed to her preservation." To his London history is added the information that before he became poet to the royal theatre he spent a year "totally destitute of employment" and then went to Holland for the purpose of establishing there an Italian theatre. He was encouraged in the project, and had almost succeeded, "when the defeat of the English under Dunkirk changed the face of affairs." He remained in his position of theatrical poet eight years, "with much profit and not without honor," he says, and then continues: "It was snatched from me by means of some female artifices at a moment when I had the least apparent reason to apprehend such a loss." What is referred to in these words is not clear. Da Ponte had the reputation of a gallant, and even in his old age could not resist the temptation to discourse on the favor in which he had stood with the fair sex and the fidelity with which he had lived up to every promise to love a woman made between the period when he first experienced the passion, at eighteen years, to the time of his marriage, when he was forty. Later in his pamphlet he refers to the money which his wife had earned by "her own honorable industry," and appends this foot-note: "Do you understand the meaning of that word, once beautiful Rossellana of England?" That he had many enemies in the theatrical circles of London is well known, and with some he carried on a bitter personal controversy. Of this fact an amusing bit of evidence is contained in a volume of miscellaneous pamphlets in the Historical Society's library. Among the pamphlets is an Italian one, printed without date and anonymously in Lisbon. It is an indecent attack on "the celebrated Lorenzo Daponte, who after having been Jew,

Christian, priest, and poet in Italy and Germany found himself to be a layman, husband, and ass in London." In this pamphlet is a sonnet addressed to Da Ponte, in which by a pun his name is associated with the Ponte Oscura, a disreputable quarter of Naples. Next to this delectable pamphlet is bound a reply, also unsigned, which bandies epithets with the alleged author of the former with a freedom and vigor which would be considered startling even by the controversialists of the far West. This is the way in which the climax is reached: *Poeta di Priapo, di Cotitto, di Petunda, di Stercuccio e di tutti le fogne, ed i Lupinari di Londra.* Again in the "Compendium," while emphasizing the statement that he brought nothing with him from England to America except " some books and a box of violin strings," he adds: " whatever may be said by the illiterate singer of Haymarket or the Delilah of the Neapolitan Eunuch." The indignant protestation, it must be confessed, sounds a little amusing in view of the fact that a few pages later he says: "A glass of wine given with affected compassion by a needy sharper on board the fatal Nantucket vessel cost me $300 more." Evidently he carried at least $300 away with him when, " pursued by twelve bailiffs," he

DA PONTE IN NEW YORK

fled from London to Gravesend, and there embarked on the Nantucket vessel, which sailed for Philadelphia on March 26, 1805, and reached New York on June 4.

His wife, he says, had been in America on a visit to her father not a year, but so long that "about the middle of February" he had sent her a peremptory injunction to return.[1] She was about to obey him when he arrived. His wife had brought over $5,000 (remember Rossellana) and soon got $1,000 more from her sister in London. With this money Da Ponte embarked in business. Evidently he was not cut out for a tradesman. In three months, through his "wonted lenity of temper," he had lost $300; then the fear of yellow fever drove him to Elizabethtown, N. J., where he bought a house and lot and continued his traffic in liquors, tobacco,

---

[1] In spite of Da Ponte's theatrical protestation that his lips had never spoken an untruth (he was a poet and much given to hyperbole), investigation of his career discloses many things which can not now be reconciled with his statements. If he had been in correspondence with his wife sometime before he commanded her to return to London from New York in February, 1805, as he says, she certainly must have been here in 1804; yet the notices of Lorenzo L. Da Ponte (son of the poet and professor of Italian in the University of the City of New York for several years prior to his death in 1840), official and otherwise, agree in saying that he was born in London in 1805.

drugs, etc. He failed, he says, because his customers did n't pay. Here is his woeful complaint: " I was sometimes obliged, rather than lose all, to take, for notes due long before, lame horses, broken carts, disjointed chairs, old shoes, rancid butter, watery cider, rotten eggs, apples, brooms, turnips, potatoes;" and these things he had to sell at a sacrifice in order to meet the demands of " creditors without mercy." Plainly Da Ponte was not a financier. In his books those who owed him money are all unconscionable scoundrels and cheats, and those to whom he owes money are all merciless, grasping skinflints who sold him bad goods. His New Jersey venture lasted a year; then he sold out, and the sheriff, prompted by a peculiarly wicked creditor, named Dunham, seized upon his household effects. He returned to New York, began to teach Italian, and entertained his first class with a sketch of his life, from which the above drafts have been made, and which included a financial showing of the Jersey business. The citizens of Elizabethtown owed him about $800; he owed $400 in New Jersey; he had $1,600, which he divided among his New York creditors, but it was "not enough to meet all demands," nor were all these demands paid

DA PONTE IN NEW YORK

after he had handed over to his creditors $3,450. Da Ponte was surely ingenuous when it came to finances.

Da Ponte now entered on a period of successful teaching in New York. His name appears for the first time in Longworth's directory for 1807.[1] The period lasted till 1811, and was distinguished each year by a change of residence; among other places, he lived at No. 29 Partition-street, in the Bowery, and at No. 247 Duane-street. Having amassed a fortune of $4,000 he again embarked in business. This time he became a distiller in Sunbury, Penn. He stayed from June 10, 1811, till August 14, 1818, and of course was more dreadfully ruined than ever

[1] If it is true that three movings are as bad as a fire, Da Ponte's local peregrinations might be cited as either cause or proof of his poverty. Investigation of the directories of New York discovers the following list of his dwelling places: 1807, No. 29 Partition-street; 1808, the Bowery; 1810, No. 247 Duane-street; 1819, No. 54 Chapel-street; 1820, No. 17 Jay-street; 1821, No. 343 Greenwich-street; 1824, No. 51 Hudson-street; 1825, No. 92 Hudson-street; 1826, No. 206 Duane-street; 1827 and 1828, No. 390 Greenwich-street; 1829 to 1835, No. 342 Broadway, with the bookstore at No. 336 (then, as now, the numbers were in the vicinity of Catherine-lane); 1836 and 1837, No. 35 Dey-street; 1838, No. 91 Spring-street, where he died. The directories of 1811 and 1823 are missing in the Trow collection, and that of 1809 is defective.

before. Again he was the only sheep in a flock of wolves. On his return he again gathered his pupils around him. He won the friendship of no less powerful an advocate than Clement Clarke Moore, whom scholars honor as the pioneer Hebrew lexicographer of the United States, and whom children love as the author of " 'Twas the Night before Christmas." His summers he spent near noble patrons, the Livingstons, on the Hudson; his winters in town. He wrote his memoirs in three small volumes, and published them in 1823. He lectured on Italy, and even measured his pen with that of Prescott, who had ventured to criticise Italian narrative poetry in "The North American Review." Exactly when does not appear, but it seems that he also taught "Aunt Sally," who kept a boarding-house in Broome-street, the art of Italian cookery, and cultivated in his pupils simultaneously the taste for Petrarch and macaroni. His friend, Clement C. Moore, was a trustee of Columbia College, and probably through his advocacy Lorenzo Da Ponte became professor of Italian literature in Columbia College, then situated at the foot of Park Place, near Broadway. The story of this professorship can be told in a few extracts from the minutes

DA PONTE IN NEW YORK

of the Trustees of Columbia College and a postscript.

From the minutes of Columbia College:

May 2, 1825. A letter from Mr. Da Ponte was received, asking permission to instruct the alumni of the College in the Italian language and to make use of some part of the building for that purpose. The above letter was referred to the Standing Committee.

June 6, 1825. (At this meeting the report of the Standing Committee was laid on the table for further consideration.)

September 5, 1825. *Resolved*, That a Professorship of Italian Literature be established in this College, but that the Professor be not considered one of the Board of the College, nor subject to the provisions of the second chapter of the statutes.

Resolved, That the attendance of the students upon the said Professor be voluntary, and that the hours of attendance be appointed by the Professor, under the direction of the President.

Resolved, That Signore Da Ponte be and is hereby appointed to the said professorship, and that he be allowed to receive from the students who shall attend his lectures a reasonable compensation; but that no salary be allowed him from the College.

December 5, 1825. (Da Ponte offers to sell two hundred and sixty-three volumes of Italian works to the college for $364.05. Referred to a committee, C. C. Moore, chairman.)

January 2, 1826. (Favorable report; the books are bought for the library.)

January 5, 1829. Ordered that $50 be paid to Signore Da Ponte in addition to what he has already been paid for making the catalogue of the College.

November 3, 1829. (Da Ponte offers more books.)

November 12, 1829. (Thirty-three volumes bought of Da Ponte for $140.)

November 30, 1829. A proposition was received through the President from Signore Da Ponte, offering to add a number of Italian books to the College Library upon condition of his having a certain number of pupils provided him to instruct in the Italian language. Whereupon —

Resolved, That it is inexpedient to accept of the proposition of Signore Da Ponte.

These are the only instances in which Da Ponte's name appears in the minutes of Columbia College. From the volume added to his memoirs in 1830 the meaning of the last entry may be learned. He was a professor without pupils or salary. His proposition was to give two lessons for forty weeks to one hundred students, each to pay $15 for

DA PONTE IN NEW YORK

the eighty lessons, and then to present one thousand volumes to the College.

The years from 1807 to 1811 and from 1818 to 1826 were evidently the only happy ones in Da Ponte's American life. Some of his pupils went to live with him at his summer home to continue their studies. Among them was Henry James Anderson, who became professor of mathematics and astronomy in Columbia College in 1825, and who married Da Ponte's daughter. Dr. Anderson remained professor until 1843, became a convert to Romanism, and died in 1875 at Lahore, India, whither he had gone on a scientific commission. His wife died in 1843 in Paris while returning with her husband from Rome. She is buried in Père la Chaise. Dr. Anderson was but once married and left only two children, Edward Henry and Elbert Ellery; the latter is a prominent lawyer of New York City, and an active Democratic politician.

The last ten years of Da Ponte's life were both brightened and clouded by efforts to introduce Italian opera in America. When Garcia came in November, 1825, with an Italian troupe including his daughter, afterward Malibran, Da Ponte was among his earliest visitors. The story of their meeting is a familiar one. Da Ponte introduced himself to the singer as the author of "Don Giovanni" ("my 'Don Giovanni,'" he was fond of saying), and Garcia, clasping him in his arms, danced about the room like a child, singing *Fin ch' han dal vino*. Naturally "Don Giovanni" was given in the first season, though Da Ponte and his "friends and pupils" had to pay an extra singer in order to have a *Don Ottavio*. Later Da Ponte associated himself with Rivafinoli in operatic management, and even succeeded in persuading some wealthy citizens to build an opera house at Church and Leonard-streets. The operatic ventures were disastrous. He wrote and published two pamphlets about the Montressor season in 1832, and in 1835 appended to a complaint of his recent sufferings a letter in which he denounced Rivafinoli, accused the public of ingratitude toward himself, and urged that the theatre be leased to one Rocco. Da Ponte went with all his troubles straight to the public through the medium of the printing press, and it makes a somewhat diverting effect in spite of his obvious seriousness to read on one page of his pamphlet an almost hysterical prayer to the stockholders of the opera house to listen to his advice and take the word " of an old man whose lips have never uttered an untruth," and on the next a warning to his debtors, threatening to sell their notes at public auction and tell the " circumstances under which they were offered and received" unless they are paid before a given day. When he records his failure to change the system of instruction at Columbia he does so cheerfully enough. He tells in the last pages of his " Memorie" that he had now opened a bookstore in front of which he could see all day long the most beautiful women in the world step out of their carriages. They were bent on the purchase of candies and cakes in the adjoining shop. Then he tells how the temptation had seized him to put up a sign in his window: " Candies and Italian cakes sold here." If by such a trick somebody shall be tempted into his store, " then," he says, " will I bring forth Petrarch, or some other of our poets, and I will vouch that they are the sweetest of all candies for those who have teeth to masticate them." But he did not always take so cheerful a view of life. It is plain from all his writings that he considered himself not appreciated at his true worth. He thought himself a genius, and since the people would not discover that fact of their own volition he kept asseverating it in his writings. Toward the end of his life the fact that he was in danger of dying neglected seems to have weighed greatly on his mind. In a letter printed in his memoirs a friend, evidently C. C. Moore, takes him to task for it. Says the letter writer:

It seems to me that you are a little too anxious in regard to the memory that you wish to leave behind you. For all that you have already done for the love of the Italian language and literature the name of Da Ponte, *clarum et venerabile nomen*, will be kept in great veneration so long as there remains in this country a taste for elegant letters, and the youth of both sexes will look back in the decline of life to the hours passed in pleasant and instructive conversation with their illustrious and elegant teacher as to the most brilliant moments of their existence. This is enough. Do not seek, like Bonaparte, to conquer for yourself all the glory of the world.

A few more extracts from the publications of his latter days evince the same spirit. In a letter set as a preface to a pamphlet which he calls " Frottola per far ridere," in 1835, he says:

Eighteen months are passed since I had a single pupil. I, the creator of the Italian language in America, the teacher of more than two thousand persons whose progress astounded Italy! I, the poet of Joseph II., the author of thirty-six dramas; the inspiration of Salieri, of Weighl, of Martini, of Winter and MOZART! After twenty-seven years of hard labor I have no longer a pupil! Nearly ninety years old, I have no more bread in America!

In a similar tone he writes to a friend in Italy: "If fate had led me to France instead of America I would not now fear that my remains might become food for the dogs; I would have earned enough money to secure rest for my old body in the grave and preserve my fame against total oblivion." In 1835, too, he published a "Storia Americana, ossia il Lamento." It is a poet's lament, a portion of which he himself translated, beginning:

Yet to the hand which has those treasures given,
Ye have refused the cymbals and the lyre;
And from *his* brow the laurel crown have riven,
Whose name has set the proudest stage on fire.
Have suffered one by cursed envy driven,
(One who, when thousands he had all bereaved
And none were left, his very self deceived,)
To bar to him the temple he had striven
With pain and toil to rear. Permitted rage
To seize the little mercy that was meant
And given by another, to assuage
The sorrows of a life so nearly spent,

A MOZART CENTENARY

That good men trembled, as with taunting scorn,
(And hate, of malice and of envy born,)
By ruthless hands *that* old man's hair was torn.
Nor will I now what I have borne declare,
My bitter wrongs, the horrors of my fate,
Through life those wrongs and horrors will I bear.
My death, what now I speak not, shall relate.
They shall declare who love the sacred NINE,
To whom I consecrate my heart and song,
They shall declare that sorrows have been mine,
And pain and silent suffering and wrong —
For this heaven's light is still to me divine,
Nor will I at the ills I bear repine.
Oh! why does reverence the right deny
To speak the names that struggle in my breast?
Those *cherished names* whose mem'ry can not die
Until this beating bosom is at rest.
Those names alone have had the power to dry
The struggling tear, and check the rising sigh.
When in the garden, beautiful and fair,
The jasmine blossomed, planted by my care,
The vi'let, the narcissus, and the rose,
The lily, type of virtue and repose,
The stately tulip and the fleur-de-lis,
Adding their beauty to the scenery,
While flowers of fairest and of richest hue,
Upon the air their sweetest perfume threw —
Spring into freshened life at my command,
Planted and raised and cultured by my hand.
When to the marsh-born magpie and the crow,
That garden's gates were ope'd but shut to me,
Those names I loved sustained me in my woe,
Checked my despair and soothed my misery.
For *them* I suffered that dogs, wolves, and all
The beasts of prey upon my flesh should fall,

DA PONTE IN NEW YORK

Drink the warm current from my bleeding heart,
And glutted, deaf to all my cries, depart.
For this I took and nurtured in my breast
A ravenous beast, more fierce than all the rest,
In form a dove, but of his plumage shorn
A dove he came at earliest dawn of morn;
I found him plumage — mark the change at night,
A serpent writhes, discovered to my sight,
Sucks the heart's fountain to the very lees,
Contemns, betrays, traduces me and flees.

I quote these lines merely for the curious interest which they possess as a specimen of the old poet's English versification, and as an evidence of the frame of mind in which he kept himself in his last years. In the English preface to the poem he relates that he had determined to return to Italy to die, when dissuaded by the receipt of a letter from an admiring benefactor, inclosing fifty dollars. He concludes as follows:

I remain. I will try to be known through the testimony of persons worthy of belief. It is my intention to publish fifty letters from distinguished persons in Europe. They are all precious to me for their contents and the names of those who wrote them; but the name of the benevolent AMERICAN DONOR is, to me, the gem of the collection, both from the moment in which it was written, and all it says. One such citizen ennobles any place. New York may boast of many such —

with her will I leave my ashes, as I have given to her thirty years of my life. Perhaps those ashes will receive, even from the ill-disposed and the ungrateful, *Vano conforto di tardi sospiri.*

Da Ponte died of old age on August 17, 1838, at 9 P. M., at his home, No. 91 Spring-street. Dr. J. W. Francis attended him, and to him the poet a day before his death, his leading passion inextinguishable, addressed a sonnet. Allegri's " Miserere " was sung at his funeral and, say eye-witnesses, he was buried " in the Roman cemetery in Second-avenue." Between Second-avenue and First at that time there were no buildings. Gulian C. Verplanck and Dr. Macneven were among his pall-bearers. The Italians of the city resolved to rear a monument over his grave, but never did so, and the place of his burial is unmarked and unknown, like the grave of Mozart.[1]

[1] The death notice in "The Evening Post," of August 18, 1838, announces the funeral of Da Ponte as to take place "to-morrow afternoon at five o'clock from his late dwelling-house, No. 91 Spring-street." As a matter of fact the funeral took place in the Cathedral at twelve o'clock of the day after the one set in the advertisement. It is probable that the friends of the dead man, desiring to show him some honors, changed the first plans of the family. Tuckerman says: "The obsequies of Da Ponte were impressive   The funeral took place at noon of the 20th of

DA PONTE IN NEW YORK

There arises naturally a curiosity as to Da Ponte's personal appearance. I have seen two portraits, one an oil painting in the

August, 1838. Allegri's Miserere was performed over his remains at the Cathedral; the pall-bearers were his countryman, Maroncelli, the companion of Pellico's memorable imprisonment at Spielberg; his old friend, Clement C. Moore, and two eminent citizens — the Hon. Gulian C. Verplanck and Dr. Macneven; on the coffin was a laurel wreath, and before it, on the way from the church to the Roman cemetery in Second-avenue (*sic.* Mr. Ward says simply 'to the Roman cemetery'), whither it was borne — followed by a long train of mourners led by the officiating priests and the attendant physician — was carried a banner, and on its black ground was this inscription:

Laurentius Daponte. Italia. Natus. Litterarum. Reipublicæ. et Musis. Dilectissimus. Patriæ. et conciorum. Amantissimus. Christianæ. Fidei. Cultor. Adsiduus. In Pace. et Consolatione. Lustrorum. XVII. Die Augusti. MDCCCXXXIII. XC Anno. Ætatis. Suæ. Amplexu. Domini. Ascendit.

A private letter from Mr. E. Ellery Anderson says: "I can not inform you as to his place of burial. He died during an absence of several months of my father from the city. Some Italian societies, I am informed, took charge of the ceremonies. He was buried in the cemetery near Eleventh-street and Second-avenue. About twenty years since my father received a communication from the authorities of Ceneda, his native village near Venice, asking information as to where he was buried. I spent several days in investigating the matter, but was unable to find any trace of him. My judgment is that his remains were placed temporarily in some friend's vault, with the intention of erecting a formal monument at a later period, and that this matter has been overlooked or forgotten until all traces of the poet's remains have been lost."

library of Columbia College, the other a steel engraving put as a frontispiece in the "Frottola per far ridere," of which mention has been made. In the painting Da Ponte sits at a writing-table with a pen in his right hand and the left clasping the top of a large book which rests on his knee. The brow is a noble one, but the face runs down to a rather pointed chin. As a whole the cast of countenance is decidedly more Hebraic than the other portrait, which, of course, was sanctioned by the original or it would not have appeared in one of his books. The latter, which was copied in the "New York Mirror" to illustrate an article on Da Ponte's death, written by Samuel Ward, is, however, in better accord with the descriptions to be found in local literature. In "Old New York," published in 1858, Dr. John W. Francis, who attended the old poet on his death-bed, speaks of him as "the stately nonagenarian, whose white locks so richly ornamented his classical front and his graceful and elegant person." Mr. Tuckerman, who seems also to have been acquainted with Da Ponte, in the article published years ago in "Putnam's Magazine" describes him thus: "At the age of ninety Lorenzo Daponte was still a fine-looking man; he had

DA PONTE IN NEW YORK

the head of a Roman; his countenance beamed with intelligence and vivacity; his hair was abundant and fell luxuriantly round his neck, and his manners combined dignity and urbanity to a rare degree."

In connection with these descriptions it is interesting to read what Michael Kelly (the Irish singer who sang at the first performance of "Le Nozze di Figaro" in Prague, and who caricatured Da Ponte in one of his own operas in Vienna) says in his "Reminiscences:"

My friend, the poet, had a remarkably awkward gait, a habit of throwing himself (as he thought) into a graceful attitude by putting his stick behind his back and leaning on it; he had also a very peculiar, rather dandyish way of dressing; for, in sooth, the abbé stood mighty well with himself and had the character of a consummate coxcomb; he had also a strong lisp and broad Venetian dialect.

BEETHOVEN AND HIS BIOGRAPHER

I
ALEXANDER WHEELOCK THAYER

WHEN Alexander Wheelock Thayer died on July 15, 1897, in Trieste, Austria, America lost a citizen who had brought her more renown in the world of music than any of her composers, performers or singers; yet he wrote no music and had only an amateur's knowledge of the art. He won his eminence by writing a biography of Beethoven which is recognized the world over as the court of last resort on all questions of fact concerning the great musician who linked together the eighteenth and nineteenth centuries. He gave to that work nearly fifty years of his life, yet left it uncompleted, to the infinite regret of all serious students of musical history. Three volumes were printed, in German translation, which brought the story of Beethoven's life down to the end of the year 1816. Eighteen years elapsed between the publication of Volume III and Mr. Thayer's death, but so brain-weary had he become from the labor of gathering, sifting and presenting the vast material contained in the work that the last ten years of his life saw no progress made in his *magnum opus*. So far as it goes, however, "Ludwig van Beethoven's Leben" is the final and authoritative account of the composer's life and labors. For the first time it places the history of Beethoven's career on a solid basis of fact, rectifying the great mass of fable and error that had grown up around it from the negligence and partisan bias of the composer's friends and earlier biographers, and bringing to light a great body of new and convincing data. Thayer's method was that of the modern German school of careful and exhaustive research as exemplified in Jahn's biography of Mozart, and Spitta's of Bach. Unlike those works, however, Thayer's "Beethoven" attempts no analysis or estimate of its subject's compositions. It is a study of the man, not of his music.

Mr. Thayer was born at South Natick, Mass., on October 22, 1817. He was graduated from Harvard College in 1843, and immediately went to work in the College library. While thus employed he formed the resolve the execution of which occupied him for the rest of his life. He went to Germany, where he lived for two years, collecting materials, studying the German language and otherwise fitting himself for the task which he had set himself. When he came back to the United States in 1852 he became a member of the staff of the "New York Tribune" newspaper; but music engrossed his attention, his health gave way, and he abandoned the profession of journalism, though he did not cease to write articles for newspapers and other journals, until he could write no more. In 1854 he went back to Europe, and saving two years which he spent in Boston, from 1856 to 1858, that country was his abiding-place till his death. The Boston interim brought him into close association with Lowell Mason, who employed him to catalogue his library. In 1858, largely supported by funds contributed by Dr. Mason and Mrs. Mehitabel Adams of Cambridge, Mr. Thayer returned to Europe. In 1862 he entered the service of the United States Legation at Vienna and three years later he was appointed United States Consul at Trieste by President Lincoln at the request of Mr. Motley and Senators Sumner and Wilson. He remained in office until October 1st, 1882, when President Cleveland removed him to make room for a man belonging to his political party. All the time that he could spare from his official duties was given to travels undertaken to gather material for the Beethoven biography.

The first fruits of Mr. Thayer's special study were given to the world in his "Chronologisches Verzeichniss der Werke Ludwig van Beethoven's," published in Berlin in 1865. The next year the first volume of the biography appeared. This, like the succeeding volumes (the second published in 1872, the third in 1879), was written in English and translated into German by Dr. Hermann Deiters of Bonn, to whom, after Mr. Thayer's death, his executor, Jabez Fox, Esq., entrusted the task of completing the work with the aid of the material gathered together by the great biographer. Since Dr. Burney made his memorable tours through Germany, France and Italy to gather material for his "General History of Music" it is doubtful if any investigator ever made such exhaustive and painstaking researches as Mr. Thayer. Like Dr. Burney, he believed that intelligence as well as merchandise capable of adulteration is seldom genuine after passing through many hands, and that it is always best to seek for infor-

ALEXANDER W. THAYER

mation at its source. He therefore sought out all of Beethoven's friends who were living in the sixth and seventh decades of this century, noted down their recollections of important occurrences in connection with the composer, and a multitude of incidents which might enable him the better to straighten out the thread of that lifestory which had been sadly tangled by the romancers who, under one pretence or another, were first in the field with books on Beethoven. This, however, was probably the least valuable of Thayer's labors; it did not compare with his researches in old archives, court records, etc., for the evidence, which, as he has presented it, leaves scarcely an important incident in Beethoven's life in doubt, but it resulted in the accumulation of a most interesting body of anecdote and description. To hear this from the lips of witnesses who are speaking from personal knowledge is to be brought nearer to the personality of the great genius than could be done by any amount of ordinary biographical writing; and so I give the following extracts from Mr. Thayer's notebooks (kindly placed at my disposal by Mrs. Fox, a niece of the biographer and his heir) without further change than a translation into English of the passages which occur in foreign languages:

January 2, 1860 — I visited General Gärten-Direktor Peter Lenné, at Potsdam, a native of Bonn. He told me (A. W. T.) that in 1812 he went to Vienna and took a letter from his father to B., also one from Father Ries. As B. heard the Bonn dialect he exclaimed, "I can understand you. You speak Bonnian (*Bönnisch*). You must be my guest every Sunday!"

"Father Ries" was the father of Ferdinand Ries, Beethoven's pupil, and, with Dr. F. G. Wegeler, author of the "Biographische Notizen über Ludwig van Beethoven," published in 1838.

August 29, 1859 — I met Musikdirektor Krenn on the Glacis, and he related me the two following anecdotes:

Hofrath Küffner told him (Krenn) that he once lived with Beethoven in Heiligenstadt, and that they were in the habit evenings of going down to Nüssdorf to eat a fish supper in the Gasthaus "Zur Rose." One evening, when B. was in a good humor, Küffner began:

K. — "Tell me frankly which is your favorite among your symphonies?"

B. (in great good humor) — "Eh! Eh! The 'Eroica.'"

K. — " I should have guessed the C minor."
B. — " No; the 'Eroica.' "

Krenn was a pupil of Ignatz v. Seyfried, and at one time he was studying B.'s seventh symphony with his master, and when they came to the place in the finale where the drums are out of harmony, Seyfried told this anecdote:

Years before they were rehearsing that work with his orchestra. When they came to this place he thought the parts were copied out incorrectly, but on referring to the score it was the same there. As carefully as possible he said to Beethoven: "Dear friend, there seems to be an error here; the kettledrums are not in tune." Beethoven flared up at once and exclaimed: "It is not intended that they shall be." Now, that Seyfried had learned to appreciate the poetic idea which underlies the music, he told Krenn, "Now I comprehend that the drums ought not to be in tune."

The passage in the finale of the seventh symphony referred to is probably the stubborn and dissonant roll on A near the close of the first portion of the movement.

The old actor Hopp told me to-day, October 28, 1859, that at the opening of the Josephstadt Theatre he was still in Baden, but that a few days later he came to Vienna, November 4, 1822. Hensler gave a dinner in the Garderobe of the J. S.

Theatre at 3 P. M., it being Hensler's *Namenstag*, Beethoven, Gläser, Bäuerle, Gleich, Meisel, Hopp and others being present. Beethoven had a seat directly under a musical clock. Gläser told Reubl, who provided the entertainment, to set the clock to the overture to "Fidelio" and then wrote Beethoven to listen, as he would soon hear it. Beethoven listened and then said: "It plays it better than the orchestra in the Kärnthnerthor."

Rust's Anecdote — Wilhelm Rust used to relate that in 1809 he was in a coffee-house in Vienna and Beethoven was there also. A French officer happening to pass, B. doubled up his fist and exclaimed: "If I, as a general, knew as much about strategy as I know about counterpoint as a composer, I'd cut out some work for you fellows!" This anecdote was told me by Wilhelm Rust, the nephew of the above.

April 29, 1860 — At Link's, where I met Hozalka. He speaks very highly of Schindler and of S.'s disinterested fidelity to Beethoven. Hozalka says that in 1820-'21, as near as he can recollect, the wife of a Major Baumgarten took boy boarders in the house then standing where the Musikverein's Saal now is, and that Beethoven's nephew was placed with her. Her sister, Baronin Born, lived with her. One evening he, Hozalka, then a young man, called there and found only Baronin Born at home. Soon another caller came and stayed to tea. It was Beethoven. Among other topics Mozart came on the tapis, and the Born asked Beethoven (in writing, of course) which of Mozart's operas he thought most of. "Die Zauberflöte," said Beethoven, and, suddenly clasping his hands and throwing up his eyes, exclaimed, "Oh, Mozart!"

As Hozalka had, as it was the fashion to do, always considered "Don Juan" as the greatest, this opinion by Beethoven made a very deep impression upon him.

At Artaria's I found two of the daily records of expense kept by Beethoven's housekeeper. They consist of two or three sheets of foolscap paper doubled together lengthwise and stitched. I had the curiosity to draw off the wine account as it is scattered among the items. Found it to be as follows:

		Fl.	x	
July 7 — Wine cost		9	20	W. W.
" 12 — White wine		4	15	
" " — Red "		5	25	
" 16 — White "		3	20	
" " — Red "		9	20	
" 23 — Red "	6 Mass, 3 *Seidel*	4	43½	
" " — White "	2 " 1 "	4	30	
" 28 — Wine		14		
August 6, 7 — Red wine, 7½ *Mass*		5	15	
" " — White "		2	22	

October 28 — Wine	2	30
" 31 — "	6	40
November 2 — Wine	3	30
" 14 — "	2	

N. B. — A florin (Fl.) or *gulden* W. W. (*Wiener Währung*) was near enough to be called a franc — about 20 or 21 cents American money. One English gallon equals 3.9680 Prussian quarts; one Austrian *Mass* equals 1.2359 Prussian quarts; one Austrian *Mass* equals 1.205 English quarts.

May 24, 1860, I called on Salis in the Nagler-Gasse, Wien. His wife was daughter of the violoncellist Willmann, and therefore niece of the Willmann — afterward Galvani — singer at Bonn, 1790-'93. (See Gerber's Lexicon.) She told me that her father had often told her that Beethoven was visibly in love with the beautiful songstress and offered his hand; but she refused him, he being "ugly and half crazy."

May 25, 1860 — Herr Salis took me to Hofsekretär Mähler, an old man, eighty-two years of age, born at Coblentz. He came to Vienna in 1803. Breuning introduced him to Beethoven. The place of introduction was in the Theater an der Wien, where Beethoven then had rooms. It was probably during the winter 1803-'04. They found Beethoven at work finishing the "Eroica." Wishing to hear him play, he sat down and played the Finale — theme, variations and fugue — and

ALEXANDER W. THAYER

when it was concluded, instead of leaving off, he continued in a free fantasia for two hours, during all which time, said Mähler, himself a composer, there was not a phrase (*Takt*, the word he used) which was faulty or which did not sound original.

May 28 — I called again on Mähler and questioned him as to the above, and find I have reported correctly. One thing, he says, particularly attracted his attention, and that was that he played with his hands so very still. Wonderful as was his execution, there was no tossing up and about of his hands, but they seemed to glide right and left over the keys, the fingers doing the work.

He told me that at the grand rehearsal of "Fidelio" the third fagott was absent, that Beethoven fussed and fidgeted about it, but that Lobkowitz treated the matter lightly — two fagotts were there and a third could make little difference, etc. Whereat B. was enraged, and after the rehearsal, on his way to his lodgings in the city, as he passed over the Lobkowitz-Platz, he could not resist going to the great door and calling out *Lobkowitzcher Esel!* ("Lobkowitzian ass.")

Upon inquiring what portrait Beethoven refers to in the letter to Mähler which I copied the other day, Mähler told me it was a picture which he painted soon after coming to Vienna, in which Beethoven is given nearly at full length, left hand resting on a lyre, right hand extended as if in a moment of musical enthusiasm he was beating time. In the background a temple of Apollo. Oh! if he could only know what had become of that picture! "Why," said I, "it is now hanging up in Widow Carl van Beethoven's room in the Josephstadt, and I have a copy of it!" So it appears that the picture which Luib gave me is a copy of one by Mähler.

Prince Josef Franz Maximilian Lobkowitz was one of the first and foremost of Beethoven's Viennese friends. He was two years younger than the composer, and an intimacy sprang up between the two men (Lobkowitz being an admirable amateur, playing the violin and violoncello and singing like an artist) very soon after Beethoven came to Vienna in 1792. His name appears in the dedications of the third, fifth and sixth symphonies, besides a number of other smaller but yet important works. He was one of the contributors to Beethoven's annuity, and died in 1816. Sir George Grove tells the story in his article on Beethoven in the "Dictionary of Music and Musicians," on the authority of Thayer's biography (Vol. II, p. 288). The portrait painted by Mähler was until five years ago in the possession of the widow of Beethoven's nephew, Carl van Beethoven, whose conduct when young embittered the last years of the master's life. Thayer's copy is in oil, and was exhibited at the opening of the Bonn Beethoven-Haus Museum in 1890. The Thayer copy is now the property of Mrs. Jabez Fox, Cambridge, Mass.

June 5, 1860, I was in Gratz and saw Hüttenbrenner (Anselm), who gave me the following particulars:

Some ten years before Beethoven's death A. H., then a young man, went to Vienna to spend a few years. He was an amateur musician and composer, and a Beethoven enthusiast, as were so many Gratz people. Dr. Joseph Eppinger introduced him to Beethoven, who, he thinks, was living at the time in a narrow street in the city — here his memory is not distinct. He remembers distinctly, however, the impression made upon him by the room — shirts, boots and shoes, books, music, all piled upon or scattered about the floor. As Eppinger introduced him Beethoven said, *Ich bin nicht werth dass Sie mich besuchen* ("I am not worth a visit from you"), and his manner proved that this was spoken from modesty.

Hüttenbrenner remembers also that it used to be said in Vienna in those days that what gave Beethoven his first reputation in Vienna was his superb playing of Bach's "Wohltemperirtes Clavier." As a specimen of his composition he once took his overture to Schiller's "Robbers" to B., who looked it through and then clapped him heartily upon the shoulder in proof of his approbation. He also confirms what I have so often heard of Beethoven's loud, hearty laughter.

In the winter of 1826–'27 his friends wrote him from Vienna that if he wished to see Beethoven again alive he must hurry up thither from Gratz. He hastened to Vienna, arriving a few days before Beethoven's death. Early in the afternoon of March 26 Hüttenbrenner went into the dying man's room. He mentioned as persons whom he saw there Stephen v. Breuning and Gerhard, Schindler, Telscher and Carl's mother. (This seems to be a mistake, i. e., if Mrs. v. Beethoven is right.) Beethoven had then long been senseless. Telscher began to draw the dying face of Beethoven. This grated on Breuning's feelings, and he remonstrated with him, and he put up his papers and left (?). Then Breuning and Schindler left to go out to Währing to select a grave. (Just after five — I got this from Breuning himself — when it grew dark with the sudden storm, Gerhard, who had been standing at the window, ran home to his teacher.) Afterward Gerhard v. B. went home, and there remained in the room only Hüttenbrenner and Mrs. van Beethoven. The storm passed over, covering the Glacis with snow and sleet. As it passed away a flash of lightning lighted up everything. This was followed by an awful clap of thunder. Hüttenbrenner had been sitting on the side of the bed sustaining Beethoven's head — holding it up with his right arm. His breathing was already very much impeded, and he had been for hours dying. At this startling, awful peal of thunder, the dying man suddenly raised his head from Hüttenbrenner's arm, stretched out his own right arm majestically — "like a General giving orders to an army." This was but for an instant; the arm sunk back; he fell back. Beethoven was dead.

Hüttenbrenner says when Himmel came Beethoven said, "I must not receive him in bed," and actually got up and put on a dressing gown to receive him with due respect.

Another talk with Hüttenbrenner — It seems that Beethoven was at his last gasp, one eye already closed. At the stroke of lightning and the thunder peal he raised his arm with a doubled-up fist; the expression of his eyes and face was that of one "defying death" — a look of defiance and power of resistance.

H. must have had his arm under the pillow. I must ask him.

I did ask him; he had his arm around B.'s neck.

Mrs. v. Beethoven says that Carl's mother could not have been present at Beethoven's death, as it was a matter of complaint with her that no news of his dying condition reached her until after all was over. Dr. Breuning also thinks she could not have been there, for he has no recollection of ever having seen either of the sisters-in-law of Beethoven.

The Mrs. v. Beethoven referred to was the widow of Nephew Carl.

June 23, 1860, I called upon Professor Höfel, in Salzburg. He related the following: In 1820 he was made professor of drawing at Wiener Neustadt. A year or two after he was one evening with Eisner (still living in Vienna) and others of his colleagues; also the Police Commissary of W. Neustadt, in the garden of the Wirthshaus "Zum Schleifen," a little way out of town. It was autumn and already dark when a constable came out and said to the commissary, *Herr Commissär, wir haben Jemand arretirt welcher uns kein' Ruh gibt. Er schreit immer dass er der Beethoven sei. Er ist aber ein Lump, hat kein Hut, alter Rock, etc., kein Aufweis wer er ist, etc.* ("Mr. Commissary, we have arrested one who will give us no peace. He keeps on yelling that he is Beethoven. But he's a ragamuffin; has no hat, an old coat, etc.; nothing by which he can be identified.")

The Commissär ordered that the man be kept in arrest until morning, *dann werden wir verhören wer er ist*, etc. ("Then we will examine him and learn who he is.") Next morning the company was very anxious to know how the affair turned out, and the Commissary said that about 11 o'clock he was waked up by a policeman with the information that the prisoner gave them no peace, and demanded that Herzog, Musikdirektor in Wiener Neustadt, be called to identify him. So the Commissary got up, dressed, went out and waked up Herzog, and, in the middle of the night, went with him to the watchhouse. Herzog, as soon as he cast eyes upon the man exclaimed, *Das ist der Beethoven!* ("That is Beethoven.") He took him home with him, gave him his best room, etc. Next day came the Bürgermeister, making all sorts of apologies. As it proved Beethoven had got up early in the morning, and, slipping on a miserable old coat, and without a hat, had gone out to walk a little. He got upon the towpath of the canal and kept on and on; seems to have lost his direction, for, with nothing to eat, he had continued on until he had brought up at the canal basin at the Unger Thor. Here, not knowing where he was, he was seen looking in at the windows of the houses, and as he looked so like a beggar the people had called a constable and arrested him. Upon his arrest the composer said, *Ich bin Beethoven* ("I am Beethoven"). *Warum nicht gar?* ("Of course, why not?") said the policeman: *ein Lump sind sie; so sieht der Beethoven nicht aus* ("You're a tramp; Beethoven does n't look so"). Herzog gave him some decent clothes, and the Burgomaster sent him back to Baden, where he was then living, in the Magistrate's state coach.

This simple story is the foundation for the fine narrative related to me as a fact in Vienna that Beethoven got into this scrape following troops from Vienna who had a sham fight near Wiener Neustadt, and taking notes for his " Wellington's Sieg " — which whole story thus goes to the ground.

Cipriani Potter to A. W. T., February 27, 1861. Beethoven used to walk across the fields to Vienna very often. Sometimes Potter took the walk with him. B. would stop, look about and express his love for nature. One day Potter asked, "Who is the greatest living composer, yourself excepted?" Beethoven seemed puzzled for a moment, and then exclaimed, "Cherubini." Potter went on, "And of dead authors?" B.— He had always considered Mozart as such, but since he had been made acquainted with Handel he put him at the head.

The first day P. was with B. the latter rushed into politics and called the Austrian Government all sorts of names. He was full of coming to England, and said his desire was to see the House of Commons. "You have heads upon your shoulders in England."

One day Mr. Potter asked Beethoven's opinion

of one of the principal pianists then in Vienna (Moscheles). *Sprechen Sie nie wieder von lauter Passagen Spieler.* ("Don't ever again talk to me of mere passage (scales) players").

Once Beethoven told Stein that some strings in his Broadwood P. F. were wanting, and caught up the bootjack and struck the keys with it to show.

July 4, 1860. Called on Grillparzer. The story of his visit to Beethoven in Hetzendorf, dining with him, and of Beethoven riding back with him to the Burgthor and then leaving money to pay the coachman is true. Beethoven at dinner went into the next room and brought out five bottles of wine; one he placed at Schindler's plate, one at his own, and three at Grillparzer's. Grillparzer says he was very temperate both in eating and drinking — never knew him except on such occasions as when all had a good time generally, to go beyond his single common bottle of common wine.

When Grillparzer was a child his family lived a summer in the same house with Beethoven in Unter Döbling. Madame Grillparzer was very fond of music and used to listen to Beethoven extemporizing. One day she stood before her own door listening when B. came rushing out and so saw her. From that time on he never played in his own room. Mad. G. sent word to him by his servant that she would lock her door to the common passage and her family should go out and in the other way. No use; B. never played more!

In the last years it was a severe task to converse with him. While one was writing answers to his questions he kept on talking and would forget the connection of what was written. Grillparzer describes him as a most kind and good-natured man, *halb verrückt* ("half crazy"), though I believe he did not use this phrase.

One day Neate was with Beethoven and while urging him to visit England mentioned the excellence of the English aurists, and was sure B. would find there some remedy for his deafness.

"No," said Beethoven, in substance, "I have already had all sorts of medical advice. I shall never be cured. I will tell you how it happened. I was once busy writing an opera "——

Neate — "Fidelio?"

B. — "No, it was not 'Fidelio.' I had a very ill-tempered *primo tenore* to deal with. I had already written two grand airs to the same text, with which he was dissatisfied, and now a third, which, upon trial, he seemed to approve and took away with him. I thanked the stars that I was at length rid of him and sat down immediately to a work which I had laid aside for those airs and which I was anxious to finish. I had not been half an hour at my work when I heard a knock at my door which I immediately recognized as that of my *primo tenore*. I sprang up from my table under such an excitement of rage that as the man entered the room I threw myself upon the floor as they do on the stage" [here B. spread out his arms and made an illustrative gesture], "coming down upon my hands. When I arose I found myself deaf and have been so ever since. The physicians say the nerve is injured."

Charles Neate was an English pianist who, out of admiration for Beethoven, went to Vienna in 1815 and made the composer's acquaintance, remaining in familiar intercourse with him for eight months. He was the first performer of Beethoven's C-minor and E-flat concertos in England. He lived to be ninety-three years old, dying on Good Friday, 1877, at Brighton. Thayer visited him many years before. If the true cause of his deafness was known to Beethoven he never betrayed the fact. It was constitutional. The story about the fall upon the floor does not tell of the cause, but only of his first observation of the malady.

II

THE BEETHOVEN MUSEUM AT BONN[1]

A MUSICAL student can not visit the Beethoven Museum at Bonn without thinking of Thayer. It is almost as much a monument to the distinguished biographer as to the incomparable genius. Without Thayer's labors, indeed, it is doubtful if the Museum would ever have come into being. More than anything else the discoveries which he made touching the antecedents of Beethoven and the musical affairs of the Electoral Court, helped to stir up that feeling of local patriotism in a small coterie of art-loving citizens in Bonn which culminated in 1888 in the purchase of the house in which the composer was born, its preservation from ruin, rescue from degradation and dedication to the lovely purpose to which it is henceforth — let us hope *in sæcula sæculo-*

[1] A large portion of this essay was published in "The Century Magazine" and is reprinted here by permission of The Century Co.

rum — to be devoted. It is singular, in view of the large infusion of sentiment in German nature, that so long a time was permitted to elapse between the death of Beethoven and the taking of these wise and pious steps. But everything is singular which concerns Beethoven. There are singular lies in most of the books that have been written about him; and even more singular truths. On his deathbed a print of the house in which Haydn was born was placed in the hands of the Titan. "Look, my dear Hummel," said he to the friend who stood at his bedside, "the birthplace of Haydn! I received it to-day as a gift and it has given me a great pleasure. A wretched peasant's hut in which so great a man was born!" Did his thoughts go back to the lowly walls which echoed his own infant cries? No one can know. He died and gave no sign. It is even doubtful whether he would have been able, had he been asked, to settle a quarrel like that which broke out ten years after his death concerning which of four houses was the one in which he was born. His parents had occupied lodgings in three houses before he was six years old. He had gone away from Bonn when he was twenty-two and he never went back. There were no domestic ties to recall him. The fulfilment of his manifest destiny required that he should live in Vienna whither he had been sent by his master the Elector of Cologne, who was an Archduke of Austria, the youngest son of Maria Theresa. Bonn forgot him until he was dead, or if it did not quite forget him, it was too much concerned with its own petty affairs to remember which of its houses had held the cradle of its greatest son. Only slowly did there dawn on the city's obtuse perceptions a realization of the share which it had in the glory created by his genius; the realization never became full and perfect until an American admirer of that genius crossed the ocean and took up the task of writing the life-story of Beethoven, the man.

I have intimated that it is to Thayer that Bonn is indebted chiefly for knowledge of the part it played in the history of Beethoven. It was the confessed purpose of the biographer to strip from his subject a mass of traditional fiction, and he has done so; but he has supplied its place with an integument of romance a hundred-fold more interesting and instructive. He has recognized that it is not enough that we interest ourselves in the facts of the artist's outward life from mere affectionate curiosity concerning his personality; the scientific spirit of the times requires that the primary purpose be to study the influences that shaped his thoughts, inspired his feelings and prompted his manner of expression. For those who wish to trace the operations of the law of heredity and find long and cumulative trains of causes for each effect, Mr. Thayer's researches are invaluable. Grandfather, father, and son, the Beethovens were in the active service of the Electoral Court in Bonn sixty years. Thayer's earliest inquiries begin with the career of the Elector Joseph Clemens, the predecessor of Elector Clemens Augustus under whom the grandfather of the composer entered the Electoral Chapel. They embrace the personal and artistic character of the potentates with the special purpose of showing what were the social and artistic influences exerted by them in the capital of their political and religious empire. His examination of the Court archives at Dusseldorf and Bonn discovered a number of documents which enable us to reconstruct a perfect picture of the art-life of the city for three-quarters of a century. The opening of the Museum in 1890 was made the occasion of an exhibition of these documents and a large collection of Beethoven relics from all over Germany. The whole partook of the character of a series of illustrations to Thayer's book. As a rule museums in which relics of the great men of the earth are preserved are little else than curiosity shops which provide entertainment for sentimental misses and hero-worshippers. The Beethoven Museum is of a different sort. As the complement of Thayer's book it is a contribution of vast significance to the history of the composer which by direct instruction and through suggestion teaches a multitude of things concerning the man and his art which can not be learned elsewhere. The correctness of this proposition is demonstrated in the story of the house itself. Beethoven was dead nearly twenty years before the antiquaries of his native town had settled a controversy touching which of several houses was the one in which he had first seen the light. More than this: Even after the fact had been determined, more than a quarter of a century was permitted to go by before there was what might be called an official recognition of the results of the controversy. When Beethoven died in 1827 there were four houses in Bonn of each of

THE MUSEUM AT BONN

which it was thought by some persons that it was the birthplace of the master.

They were respectively in the Rheingasse, Wenzelgasse, Auf der Brücke and Bonngasse. It required but little investigation, however, to narrow the question to two houses, that in the Rheingasse near the river, No. 934 (it has since been demolished and the house which is still occasionally shown to visitors as Beethoven's birth-house is a new one on the old site) and that in the Bonngasse, old number 515, new number 20, near the market-place in the centre of the town. The former house was generally accepted as the true one for more than a decade after Beethoven died. It was so described in the guidebooks and it seemed as if the majority of the residents who remembered the great man as a child associated him with the house. It was chiefly due to Dr. Wegeler, one of the friends of Beethoven's youth, that the claims of the Rheingasse house were disallowed and the truth was established that the Beethoven family were living in the Bonngasse in 1770. This was accomplished in a controversy carried on in the "Cölnische Zeitung" in 1838. There seemed to be no official record to which appeal could be made except the register of baptisms. This showed that Beethoven had been christened in the parish of St. Remy (Latin, *Remigius*) on December 17, 1770. It being the custom to baptize children in the parish where they were born it followed that Beethoven was born in the parish of St. Remy. On this the champions of the house in the Rheingasse placed their chief reliance, for their street had the proper parochial relation, while the Bonngasse throughout its length belonged to the parish of St. Peter in Dietkirchen. The evidence, supported as it was by the testimony of an elderly spinster who lived in the house all her life and was eight-and-one-half years older than Beethoven, and who said she distinctly remembered seeing him as a babe lying in his cradle, and also as a child standing on a foot bench before the pianoforte, would have been conclusive had not Dr. Wegeler been able to prove that Bonn had undergone an ecclesiastical reorganization in 1806 when under French rule which took the Bonngasse out of the parish of St. Remy and put it in the parish of St. Peter in Dietkirchen. This he did by the aid of an aged ex-mayor of the city and a parish priest who had belonged to St. Remy before the re-districting was accomplished.

THE MUSEUM AT BONN

Having thus disposed of his opponents' syllogism by proving the falsity of its minor premise Dr. Wegeler brought forward certified copies of three lists of subscribers, resident in the two streets, to a fund for the building of a parochial house in the parish of St. Remy. The lists were dated 1769, 1770, and 1771. The name of Beethoven's grandfather appears on the first and third with his official designation as chapel-master, and the name of "Herrn van Beethoven" on the second; in every case as residents in the Bonngasse. The "Herrn van Beethoven" was obviously the father of the composer, since the name is unaccompanied by a title, he being only a tenor singer in the Electoral Chapel of which his father was director. There is no Beethoven in the Rheingasse list, though the name of the then owner of the house, a baker named Fischer, father of the spinster who thought she remembered baby Louis in his cradle, appears. The disagreements were afterward cleared away by proof that the Beethoven family occupied lodgings in the house in the Rheingasse for a space after 1775. The babe in the cradle was a younger brother of the composer, born there. A brother of the spinster Cæcilia Fischer, named Gottfried, was moved by the controversy to write down his childhood recollections, and family traditions, intending to publish them in book-form. He was born ten years later than Beethoven, and in 1838 was a master baker. Literary ability he had none, and his document grew into a rambling affair full of reiteration and historical details drawn from various sources, to which he made additions down to 1864. But though its contention touching the birth-place of the composer was disproved, it is an extremely interesting contribution to the history of Bonn and the Beethoven family, and is now one of the treasures of the Beethoven Museum.

The controversy which had been provoked by a review of Wegeler's "Biographical Notices" was summarized by the Secretary of the Committee under whose auspices in 1845 the Beethoven monument was placed in the Münsterplatz; but despite the magnitude of the celebration which attended the unveiling of the statue no steps were taken to mark the house. The tablet now to be seen upon its front was not affixed until 1870, the centenary of Beethoven's birth. As late as 1886 I was invited by an occupant of the house which now stands on the old site in the Rheingasse to enter and inspect the room in which Beethoven was born. The old tradition, maintained by the thrifty desire to earn a *Trinkgeld*, "died hard," but it received its quietus when the house in the Bonngasse was bought by the Verein Beethoven-Haus in 1889 and the lying tablet on the house in the Rheingasse was removed to make place for one bearing an inscription in harmony with the facts.

For nearly one hundred years after Beethoven left Bonn, the house in which he was born was permitted to remain private property, and no steps were taken to protect it against ignoble uses. Had it been turned into a brothel the municipal authorities might have undertaken its regulation, but as its abuse did not reach that extreme they felt no concern about it. The point at which it stopped in its descent towards infamy was only a little short of that suggested. The house was for a time used as a beer-shop, and in the little rear garden the owner built a sort of summer house in which he gave concerts of a low order. The windows of the garret room in which the greatest tone-poet that the world has produced was born (the family occupied only the rear portion of the building) looked out on what the Germans call a *Tingeltangel*. To make the degradation of the spot complete the manager was wont to advertise his concerts as taking place "in the house in which Beethoven was born." The last programme containing this announcement is one of the curious possessions of the Museum. In 1889 the house was bought by a society organized for its preservation for about $14,000 — relatively an exorbitant sum, exacted by a conscienceless owner who knew the object of the purchasers, and utilized the advantage which his knowledge gave him. The first efforts of the society were directed towards its renovation and the removal of all additions which had been made in the century. The concert-saloon was torn down and the old aspect of the garden restored; show windows which had been built into the street-front were removed, and a modern pair of stairs was replaced by the original stairs with wrought iron rail which had luckily been stowed away in a storeroom. The floors, doors and ceilings in the rear house were thought to be original, and were left unchanged beyond necessary repairs. Every bit of wood of which it could reasonably be believed that it was part of the house in the time of Beethoven was piously preserved, and Mr. William Kuppe,

THE MUSEUM AT BONN

a musician largely instrumental in calling the enterprise into existence, told me with much amusement of the suspicions touching his mental condition which he aroused in the minds of the workmen, when he carefully wrapped the threshold of the birth-room in paper, carried the well-worn, worm-eaten piece of wood away till the work of renovation was finished, and then insisted upon its being replaced. In May, 1890, the museum was opened to the public with the exhibition of relics already mentioned, and a festival of Beethoven's chamber music, in which the chief performer was Joseph Joachim, the Honorary President of the society.

Of the articles exhibited at that time many have remained in the possession of the society. It is my purpose to speak of only a few of them which serve markedly to illustrate the educational value of the institution. Prominent among these is the portrait of the mother of the composer, which was never publicly exhibited before 1890, though for a long time before then in the possession of a collector of Bonn. Belief in its authenticity is based chiefly on an uninterrupted tradition reaching back through the century, and its correspondence with the description of her personal appearance in the Fischer manuscript: "Stature of Madame van Beethoven rather large; longish face; nose a little bent; spare; earnest eyes." She was a native of Ehrenbreitstein and her father was chief cook in the service of Caspar Wenzelaus, the Elector of Treves. This fact in a manner connects the story of the composer with an interesting episode in the career of Prince-Bishop Clemens Augustus — the culminating incident in that career indeed. Of Clemens Augustus, Thayer says that he "literally danced himself out of this world into the next." It is extremely likely (evidence on this point is not forthcoming, however) that when he accomplished this feat the father of Beethoven's mother was on hand to see. It was in 1761 that on his way to Munich the Elector of Cologne stopped at Castle Ehrenbreitstein to visit his brother in Church and State, the Elector of Treves. There he fell ill and was unable to partake of the dinner which the chief cook, who may have been Beethoven's maternal grandfather, had provided. But if he could not eat, neither could he withstand the charms of the Baroness Waldendorf, sister of his august and very reverend host. To her he gave his episcopal and electoral hand for not less than nine dances. Not to be thought wanting in gallantry to others of the fair he forgot the need of moderation, fell in a swoon, and was carried to his chamber, where he died next day. The spectacle of an Archbishop dancing himself to death through admiration of a pretty woman, though calculated to make us marvel to-day, was not so singular a century or two ago. Their vows sat lightly upon many of the men who exercised a double despotism by reason of their headship in both church and state. Most of them were prelates only in authority and name. Joseph Clemens, the uncle and predecessor of Clemens Augustus, was a Bavarian prince. A papal dispensation enabled him to postpone the taking of holy orders for seventeen years after he entered upon his office. How much appreciation of the sanctity of the priesthood he felt is illustrated in a story which tells how once, while an exile in Valenciennes (he had espoused the wrong side of the war about the Spanish succession and his army had fallen foul of Marlborough), he announced a purpose to preach a sermon on the approaching first day of April. When the time came the church was thronged by the faithful. Clad in the sacred vestments and greeted by the joyous noise of trumpets the Archbishop climbed into the pulpit.

BEETHOVEN

Gravely he bowed his head, decorously made the sign of the cross, then shouted "April fool!" and withdrew in pomp from the presence of his astounded congregation. Of this Prince-Bishop it is related that after he had been consecrated by the saintly Fénelon, he attested the sincerity of his piousness by never giving audience to the mother of his children save in the presence of witnesses. His nephew, who made the saltatorial exit from life's stage, never found it necessary to resort to so burdensome a formality. He was content to yield up a place in the heart of his mistress to his minister, Belderbusch, and the minister requited the kindness by assuming the paternity of the children in the case. The lady was not only a countess but also an abbess, and she and the minister were the godparents of a younger brother of Beethoven's, Caspar Anton Carl.

I seem to have digressed, but perhaps the brief sidewise excursion will be pardoned for the sake of the light which it throws upon some of the social influences which were in force in Bonn during the early stages of Beethoven's life-history. These influences seem to have left his paternal grandfather and his mother untouched. If it be true that the cause of Beethoven's deafness was an inherited disorder, they may be said to have contributed indirectly to the misfortune which embittered his life. But this is matter only for scientific speculation. Yet if it be so it serves to throw into higher relief the nobility of his character, the chastity of his mind, and the purity of his life. It also accounts for his life-long reverence and love for the memory of his grandfather (who died when he was a child), and for that of his sweet, patient, suffering mother. To her we must recur for a moment. Her maiden name was Maria Magdalena Keverich. Before she was seventeen years old she was married to Johann Laym, a servant of the Elector of Treves, who left her a widow before she was twenty. She was married to Johann van Beethoven, tenor singer in the Chapel of the Elector of Cologne at Bonn, on November 12, 1767, and died of consumption at the age of forty-one years. Her last sickness hastened the return of Beethoven from his visit to Vienna in 1787. The portrait of her in the museum is supposed to be the work of Casper Benedict Beckenkamp, also a native of Ehrenbreitstein and like the chief-cook Keverich also in the service of the Elector of Treves.

The portrait of Beethoven's mother, assuming it to be such, is the most valuable contribution which the museum has made to this branch of Beethoveniana. It has a rival in interest, however, in the picture of the Countess Brunswick. This has long been known to the *cognoscenti*, but it has acquired a new and special value of late years from the fact that investigators, acting on a hint thrown out by Thayer, have at last identified the Countess as the "immortal beloved" of the passionate love-letters by Beethoven, long but falsely believed to have been written to the Countess Guicciardi. There can now be little doubt that the Countess Brunswick was the other party to the mysterious betrothal of which so much has been said.

The collection of over a hundred paintings, prints, casts, etc. of Beethoven now in the museum serve a double purpose by directing attention at once to the few authentic portraits of the composer in existence, and to the wideness and wildness of the flights in which artistic fancy has indulged in trying to produce his counterfeit presentment. There are exceedingly few pictures in existence which were made in Beethoven's youth and early manhood.

It was only after he became famous in Vienna that artists were eager to paint him,

THE MUSEUM AT BONN

and he was to the end uncontrollable in the matter of sittings. The only full and fair opportunity which he ever gave to a good artist was in 1814 when he agreed to sit a few times to enable Blasius Höfel to correct some defects in a pencil drawing made two years before by Latronne, a French artist. This drawing was an engraving on copper for the publisher Artaria. Beethoven sat in pose for about five minutes, then rushed to his pianoforte and began improvizing. The poor engraver was at his wits' end, but was relieved of his embarrassment by the composer's servant, who told him to take a position near the instrument and work as long as he pleased, as Beethoven had entirely forgotten him and did not know that any one was in the room. Höfel took the advice and made so much progress with his plate that its completion required only two more sittings of less than an hour each. He left the room without the knowledge of the composer. Beethoven always esteemed this portrait highly, and in 1815 sent a copy of it to his friend Wegeler in Bonn. Its excellence is strongly confirmed by comparison with the cast of Beethoven's face made in 1812 by Franz Klein, a Viennese sculptor. All the strong characteristics of the mask are reproduced in the engraving — the magnificently rounded forehead, broad cheek-bones, unlovely nose and unyielding mouth — though it must be confessed with some loss in ruggedness. In the mask made by Danhauser two days after death, the marks of the mutilations made by the surgeons for the purposes of the autopsy, the organs of hearing having been removed in the hope of learning the cause of his deafness, are too evident to make contemplation anything but sorrowful. The tiny silhouette which holds a place of honor in the museum and is comparatively little known is not only the earliest of all Beethoven portraits, but the only one of unquestioned authenticity dating back to the Bonn period. It shows him in Court dress, peruke and ruff as he appeared when on duty as member of the Electoral Chapel. It was made in 1789 or 1790 by a painter named Neesen in the house of the von Breuning family where Beethoven was a frequent visitor before he went to Vienna. The house is now the home of Hermann Neusser, one of the founders of the Verein Beethoven-Haus. The singularly youthful aspect of the features shown in the silhouette is to me inexplicable. Beethoven was at the time eighteen or nineteen years old. In the familiar pen-sketch

THE MUSEUM AT BONN

by the painter and novelist Lyser, Beethoven's contemporaries were wont to praise the correctness of the attitude and carriage. This judgment now finds confirmation in the memoirs of Gottfried Fischer which mention the fact that already as a lad Beethoven bent forward when walking. The uncontested genuineness of the portrait of 1808 painted by W. J. Mähler is its chief commendation.

For nearly a century the world has tried to solve the riddle propounded by an inscrutable Providence when it permitted Beethoven to become deaf. Among the objects in the Museum are those most pitiful memorials of the physical calamity which overtook the man and musician Beethoven, the ear-trumpets and pianoforte with whose help he strove so long and so hopelessly to remain in communion with the world of sound. The pianoforte was specially made for him by Graf of Vienna. Its peculiarity is that through the greater part of its compass it has four unisonal strings for each key. So long as he could be made to hear a tone Beethoven improvized upon this instrument. But under what distressful circumstances! Maelzel, the mechanician who invented and made the ear-trumpets for him, built a resonator for the pianoforte. It was somewhat in the shape of those prompters' boxes which we see in the theatres of Germany, and was placed on the instrument so that it covered a portion of the sounding-board and projected over the keys. Seated before the pianoforte, his head all but inside the wooden shell, one of the ear-trumpets held in place by an encircling brass band, Beethoven would pound upon the keys till the strings jangled discordantly with the violence of the percussion, or flew asunder with shrieks as of mortal despair. Though the ear-trumpets had been useless for five years, they were kept in Beethoven's study till his death. Then they found their way into the Royal Library at Berlin where they remained until Emperor William II presented them to the museum. The smallest one was used by Beethoven oftenest and for the longest time. Maelzel made the instruments for Beethoven at the time when the two were contemplating a visit to London. The inventor intended to exhibit his panharmonicon, and Beethoven composed for it the descriptive piece called "Wellington's Victory" in imitation of the battle pieces which were at the height of their popularity then and still maintain themselves on and beyond the periphery of our musical communities. The projected tour was never made, and the scheme ended in a quarrel and lawsuit for which the blame was thrown on Maelzel though the fault was the composer's. A year before Beethoven died Maelzel came to America, where he remained until his death in 1838. Here, as in Europe, he depended for a livelihood on exhibitions of his mechanical contrivances, and though the biographers down to Thayer have maligned his character, he left an excellent reputation, especially in Philadelphia, where he lived longest. One of his masterpieces of mechanism was a forerunner of Ajub, the chess-playing automaton.

What shall be said at the end of the nineteenth century of him who was the musical glory of its beginning? The question can not be answered without a preliminary inquiry into the influence which deafness exerted upon his artistic character. Half a century ago the features of Beethoven's art which are now looked upon by many as evidences of progress were considered mournful aberrations due to loss of the sense of euphony and the development of an unlovely egotism which chose to assert itself in a disregard of recognized law. It is scarcely worth while now to discuss to what extent the critics of his time and a few decades after were right. There has been a marvellous change in the point of view. Other times, other manners. It is possible now — it was not possible then — to see that in Beethoven music accomplished one cycle of growth and started out on another. Starting from simple expressions of feeling which at first were unvolitional and therefore truthful but crude, it has passed through a period of mixed scientific and æsthetic development which lifted it to the dignity of an art, and enabled it to give keen gratification to the ear and the faculty of taste. In the process of this development a portion of its mission had been forgotten, though there were at all times men who apprehended and strove to promote it. Beethoven was not only the embodiment of all that was before him, but also of that which was yet to come. In his works music returned to its original purpose with its power raised a hundred-fold. It is possible, — nay more it is extremely likely, — that what seemed to him and the world the greatest evil was in fact the highest good. His deafness, while it changed his social instincts, left his moral nature unharmed.

THE MUSEUM AT BONN

If it drove him away from companionship with man it drew him closer to nature. If it hushed the amiable sounds of the external world, it also shut out some of its turmoils and enabled him the better to hear the whisperings of his own soul. Many of his admirers have found comfort in this reflection without thinking how inevitable was the consequence to his art. I can only suggest a line of thought which may bring some of the results to the mind of the reader. Macaulay, in his demonstration that the poetry of young civilizations is the best poetry, says that the progress of refinement rarely supplies music, painting, sculpture and poetry — the last least of all — with better objects of imitation. At best this is a hasty generalization. Music has as little association with the other arts in respect of its contents as it has in respect of its materials. It has in its best and true estate no object of imitation, and because of this, as well as for other reasons, it stands isolated from all the other products of the human mind. On the one hand are the things which are projected, grasped, comprehended by the intellect; on the other in awe-inspiring solitude, outside the domain of reason and therefore beyond its reach, stands music, bodying forth "the forms of things unknown." It is a pure expression of the will, the most individual, the most lawless of the arts and the one most subject to change. Its very existence is transient and contingent upon the recurrent and harmonious coöperation of three factors: creator, interpreter and hearer.

> Consider it well, each tone of one scale in itself is nought,
> It is everywhere in the world, loud, soft and all is said.
> Give it to me to use: I mix it with two in my thought
> And — there! Ye have heard and seen. Consider and bow the head.

Unperformed music is nothing, and with each act of performance there goes a new act of creation. The activities, physical, intellectual and emotional, which the three factors must exercise if music is to be at all must touch hands; yet they can not be identical. What is cause in the first case, is purpose in the second and effect in the third. Creation does not stop with the composer as it does with the painter, sculptor or architect; it is carried over to the interpreter whose work is not exposition merely but re-creation. It is this fact which entitles the instrumental performer or the singer to the name of artist. He cannot bring the crea-

THE MUSEUM AT BONN

tion of the composer to the apprehension of the hearer without blending with it something of himself. Upon the hearer, finally, devolves the duty of perceiving with the ear, judging with the intellectual and æsthetic faculties and enjoying with all these media plus the emotions; and this complicated activity is again in a high sense re-creative. It is because of this common element in the work of composer, performer and hearer that the body of music which one generation bequeaths to its successor is comparatively so small. We do not persist in creating what we do not like. Every composer is kept in court for daily judgment until the inevitable changes in taste, which follow the equally inevitable variations in percipience, relegate him to oblivion or the closed pages of history. To Beethoven music was not only a manifestation of the beautiful, — an art, — it was akin to religion. He felt himself to be a prophet, a seer. All the misanthropy, engendered by his unhappy relations with mankind, could not shake his devotion to this ideal which had sprung from the truest artistic apprehension and been nurtured by enforced introspection and philosophic reflection.

It may be — we cannot yet say — that he

went too far, that he failed to recognize the limitations which the materials of music set for the art; but there can be no doubt that he started it on the only paths along which progress was possible. Many of the things which gave offence to the taste of his time, and the first decade after, are as inexcusable now as they were then if we set it up as an inexorable maxim that the ear must always be pleased. But that conception of the aim of music is as narrow as were the rules of formal construction which he was faulted for violating. We know now that change of form is not destruction, but that in art the vessel must conform to its contents. The seemingly false entry of the horn in the first movement of the "Heroic" symphony, the rhythmical and melodic distortion of the concluding measures of the *Allegretto* of the symphony in A major, the crashing discord composed of all the tones of the minor scale in the instrumental introduction to the last movement of the "Choral" symphony are not to be set down as beauties *per se;* they derive their justification from their significance which, in turn, is to be found in the emotional and poetical contents of the works in which they occur. For the conception of characteristic beauty as opposed to the old

THE MUSEUM AT BONN

conception of absolute beauty Beethoven stood sponsor. Whither will it lead us? We cannot tell, nor will those be able to answer who shall listen to the music of a century hence. The limits of music have not been set, and can not be set. Music is the freest mode of expression open to the imagination, and Ruskin tells us

while as it penetrates into the nature of things, the imagination is pre-eminently a beholder of things as they are, it is, in its creative function, an eminent beholder of things when and where they are not; a seer, that is, in the prophetic sense, calling the things that are not as though they were; and forever delighting to dwell on that which is not tangibly present.

REFLECTIONS IN WEIMAR

THE INFLUENCE OF GOETHE AND LISZT

WEIMAR ceased to be specifically a musical Mecca with the departure of Liszt. I fancy that if some of its secret archives were thrown open to literary students, especially those who still find Goethe an interesting subject for study, it might for awhile become a literary Mecca; but in spite of its idyllic park, it has been neglected by tourists of late years and only historical interest is ascribed to it by the travelling newspaper correspondent. It is scarcely necessary to say that things were not always thus. During two periods in its history, both long, both eventful and both big with significance in the development of two intimately related arts, the little town held the attention of the world as cities with twenty times its population, forty times its wealth and a hundred times its commercial and political importance could not hold it. To-day it lives chiefly on the memories of those golden eras; and if those memories were not so perennial in their beauty and inexhaustible in their educational value, the persistence with which they are forced upon the attention of the visitor would be horribly oppressive. This is especially true of the first and most glorious era, that of which the Grand Duke Charles Augustus was the Pericles, and which was illuminated by light from the minds of Goethe, Schiller, Herder and Wieland. He who comes to Weimar now with the ordinary equipment of the tourist — Baedecker, umbrella and ostrich-appetite for relics of the great dead — can still find occupation for a day or two; but he must be panoplied in good-nature, and patience must wrap him about like a garment, if he wishes to avoid being thrown into a high fever by the appeals which will be made to him to inspect places and things hallowed to the local mind by association with Goethe. Though he come for the very purpose of putting himself as much as possible in touch with the intellectual activities which have been felt as a direct influence from the mind of the last poet of antique greatness, he shall find it difficult at times to avoid paraphrasing the remark made by Mark Twain to his Italian guide when he requested him to lump the matter of his disquisition and say that God Almighty made the world "after designs by Michelangelo." Goethe is as pervasive in Weimar as Buonarotti in Rome.

A splendid row of volumes containing the programmes, almost complete, of the performances given at the Theatre and Opera House at Weimar from 1793, two years after Goethe became its artistic director, down to to-day, is preserved in the Grand Ducal Library. In them the starting-point for many a discourse on the drama, spoken and sung, might be found. The most timely of all would perhaps suggest itself if after a perusal of their contents one were to go over to the Theaterplatz and take a look at the modest play-house which has figured so proudly in the history of the stage. For more than a quarter of a century Goethe swayed the artistic fortunes of the institution — from 1791 to 1817. For a decade, forty years later, Franz Liszt was the soul of its operatic department. During the first period the classical German drama was wrought into its perfect form; verse triumphed over prose as a vehicle of artistic utterance; Goethe and Schiller told the actors how they wanted their lines read, and even attempted to act in the parts created by them; all Germany studied the traditions of Weimar. In the second period the preeminence which the theatre enjoyed was transferred from its dramatic to its musical department. There Liszt, having withdrawn from a career as a virtuoso at the meridian of its effulgence, expended his wonderful powers in behalf of the classical masters and the gospel of the neo-romantic art. Toward Weimar the great fugitive Wagner turned his face from his Swiss asylum and longed to be among those who heard the first strains of "Lohengrin." Most pitifully did he implore Liszt, who had undertaken the task of converting the world to belief in the new evangel, to bespeak protection from his great friend and patron the grandson of that Grand Duke who knew how to fasten Goethe to his side for fifty-six years, so that he, the political outcast, might visit Weimar in disguise but for one night and hear in fact the strains to which he had so long listened in fancy.

But it was not Wagner alone for whom the unselfish Liszt made propaganda while Chapel-master Extraordinary at Weimar. Berlioz's "Benvenuto Cellini," Schumann's "Genoveva," Raff's "King Alfred," Schubert's "Alfonso and Estrella" and Cornelius's "Barber of Bagdad," besides many other works of younger or less renowned composers, all saw the light of the stage-lamps in this secluded theatre. Yet when Goethe administered the affairs of the Court Theatre, Weimar had only ten thousand inhabitants; and when Liszt made the Court Opera the heart of musical Germany, sending out from it the rich, red, arterial blood which the country needed, the institution cost less in a year than the Metropolitan Opera House in New York costs in a month. This points out the great lesson which is enforced by the history of the Weimar Theatre in its two periods of glory: true culture is dependent neither on fashion nor on wealth.

I have taken the trouble to look a little into the financial history of the institution. The theatre had existed in one form or another for a long time, when, at the suggestion of Goethe, it was raised to the dignity of a Court Theatre in 1791. The orchestra was established in 1756 by the Grand Duke Ernst Augustus, father of Goethe's patron. This Grand Duke, like many of Germany's royalties, had been musical in his youth. He was a pupil of Johann Ernst Bach, and reckoned a good player on the viol da gamba and lute. Later in life, he grew too fond of hunting and fighting, and maintained only a hunting band of pipers; but when he made Weimar his residence he established a court orchestra and called his old teacher from Eisenach to be chapel-master. The band numbered twenty men, among them being Johann Casper Vogler, who by the confession of Johann Sebastian Bach was his greatest pupil. The orchestra has been maintained ever since, and has had men like Hummel and Chelard among its conductors, though it never attracted attention as a concert body save under Liszt. This, however, is aside from my purpose, which is to show how economically Weimar's illustrious theatre has been run. In Goethe's time the receipts at the performances in Weimar, Lauchstadt and Rudolstadt averaged eleven thousand thalers; the grand ducal subvention was seven thousand thalers for the theatre and six thousand thalers to pay the orchestra; in all, twenty-four thousand thalers, or about $18,000 in American money. And this sum sufficed to meet all expenses, for it is of record that no supplementary contribution from the privy purse of Charles Augustus was ever called for during Goethe's administration. A generation later the subvention had been raised to twenty-one thousand thalers for the theatre, and twelve thousand thalers for the orchestra, but the receipts were only one thousand thalers more, and the Grand Duke was called on to pay a deficit of ten thousand thalers. To understand the modesty of these figures it is necessary to know that the theatre seats only one thousand persons, and that the prices of admission during all these palmy days ranged from twelve and a half to seventy-five cents. On ordinary subscription nights it was possible to take in only one hundred and fifty thalers at these rates, and when Sontag sang for the first time in Weimar and the prices were raised two and a half times, the receipts were yet less than twelve hundred thalers, say about $800 in the United States.

Of course all this presupposes a vastly different state of things from what our theatres and opera houses are accustomed to. In Goethe's day the play was the thing, and not its clothes. He found it as little necessary as Shakespeare to rely on gaudy trappings and adornments. In his loft were scenes depicting a forest, a city, a few rooms, a rocky landscape, and a temple. They were not many, nor even well painted, but they sufficed. "Iphigenia," "Tasso," "Faust," "Don Carlos," "The Robbers," could be played with their aid. The entire company, lyric as well as dramatic, numbered only twenty-one men and women. Sometimes the principals had to appear in two parts, and the members of the dramatic company were obliged, under their contracts, to sing in the operas. Even the costumer and carpenter had to make themselves as useful and ornamental as possible on the stage. When Mozart's operas were given the chorus was recruited from pupils of the Teachers' Seminary, and simple dances were executed by the children of court officials and private citizens. This draft on the pupils of the seminary gave rise to a somewhat acrimonious controversy between Herder and Goethe. Herder had under his care the educational as well as religious institutions of the Duchy. He had long complained about the neglect of study caused by the pupils' attendance on rehearsals at the theatre, when one day, at a performance of "Don Giovanni," the red cloak of one of the little imps that had come to carry the wicked hero to the realms of Pluto got caught in a trap. The imp was, of course, one of the seminarians. Herder thought that the cause of education was brought into ridicule by the amused laughter of the audience at the awkward mishap. He sent a protest to the Grand Duke against the further use of pupils at the theatre and argued with great force that the influence of this unnatural union of theatre and school was demoralizing to the latter. Goethe, mindful only of his beloved theatre, took arms against him and had his own way, just as a little later he persuaded Charles Augustus to give one of the theatre musicians charge of the church music, though he was a Frenchman and a Catholic and knew nothing of the institution given into his care. Again Herder complained bitterly, but in vain, and the righteousness of his position was not made plain until the experiment had proved a failure and the mischief he feared had been done.

It suggests a singular commentary on human nature, even grand ducal human nature, that though Goethe's influence was powerful enough to persuade Charles Augustus to mar the work of so illustrious a man as Herder in a department of government in which the equally great preacher and scholar stood pre-eminent, it was not great enough to withstand the combined assaults of a prima donna and a poodle dog. But the prima donna was the Grand Duke's mistress ("companion of my moments of recreation," he called her) and the dog was the progenitor of that talented race, some of whose members are still popular in the Bowery theatres. He was a "star" performer who came in April, 1817, with his master from Vienna to exhibit a historical, romantic drama translated from the French, entitled "The Dog of Aubri de Mont-Didier." Goethe objected to the engagement, but the Grand Duke granted the request of Fräulein Jagemann, who had long ruled the theatre and opera, and ordered the pair from Vienna to display their talents. There seems to be no question but that the poodle played his part brilliantly throughout three long acts. He pulled the bell-rope at a tavern door, carried a lantern into the forest at a critical point in the plot, discovered the murderer of his master, pursued him from rock to rock and attacked him with a rage that was only half simulated, for it was thought for awhile that the poor actor who had the unamiable part of murderer to play was really in danger of his life from the dog's attack. Yet Goethe, who seems to have forgotten that he had developed *Mephistopheles* out of a poodle in his great dramatic poem, remained obstinately blind to the moral and intellectual grandeur of the performance. The play was given twice, on April 12 and 14, 1817, with uproarious success, and on April 17 Goethe resigned the artistic direction of the Weimar Court Theatre. And Fräulein Jagemann got a title and estates as Frau von Heygendorf.

A portrait of Fräulein Jagemann hangs in the Grand Ducal Library. It was evidently painted at a time when she had begun to put on matronly proportions. Inasmuch as she survived Charles Augustus full twenty years and died at the age of about seventy in 1848, the picture is probably the counterfeit presentment of her as she appeared between her fortieth and fiftieth year. It shows her in the character of *Sappho*, with Greek robe and lyre. If the tale of Charles Augustus's infatuation and the many contemporaneous records were not on hand to attest the fact, this portrait would yet prove that she was a woman of extraordinary beauty. In spite of the somewhat too generous upholstery of integument, the Greek lines of her profile are still to be seen, and the faint reflection of what must have been a peculiarly lustrous and speaking pair of eyes. Her talent seems to have been commensurate with her beauty, for the programmes show that she took part in comedy, tragedy and opera, and the judgment of the time is that she was equally great in all departments. Musically, her gifts shone brightest in Mozart's operas, and in the spoken drama her principal parts were *Maria Stuart, Thekla, Portia* and *Iphigenia*.

It is through this brilliant woman that we of to-day, prone to look back upon an artistic institution which felt the direct influence of men like Goethe and Schiller and enjoyed a renown almost without parallel in the history of the stage with a feeling of awe, are privileged also to see that in those classic days of the German drama there was also present the alloy of weak human nature. Brilliant as this Demoiselle Jagemann was, I have yet to learn that Goethe ever sang her praises. The episode of "The Dog of Aubri de Mont-Didier" tells part of the story. It was the culmination of twenty years of effort to acquire complete mastery of the theatre. She was a prima donna like many prima donnas of to-day. Tears and hysterics marked her triumphant path. Her unfortunate colleagues were despoiled of their best rôles the moment she lusted after them, and the stage manager stood ceaselessly upon the treadmill of perplexity. Once, it was in 1801, an unhappy conductor thought he knew more than she about the proper tempi of *Donna Anna's* airs in "Don Giovanni." A quarrel in the rehearsal left each determined to choose the time. At the performance the conductor, Kranz, used the advantage which the bâton gave him. Jagemann quit singing, burst into tears and left the stage. Of course she appealed to the Grand Duke, with whom each saline drop weighed more than all the eloquent arguments of the musician. Poor Kranz was suspended from office, and when later he was permitted to resume his functions, it was with the condition that he should never conduct when Jagemann sang.

Nevertheless a glory which Jagemann never won with all her beauty, talent and influence was garnered by one who had preceded her on Weimar's stage, and whose portrait also hangs, a legacy from Goethe, in the library at the other end of the room which contains Charles Augustus's "*Sappho.*" The picture shows the features of Corona Elizabeth Wilhelmine Schroeter, and is doubly interesting from the fact that it was painted by its subject and presented to Goethe as a souvenir of an occasion when she had been made happy by the privilege of participating with him in one of his own plays. To have been admired, perhaps loved, by the greatest poet of his time, and one of the handsomest men, is enough in the opinion of the impressionable German maiden of to-day to give any woman a claim on immortality. The claim is recognized as valid only in the case of a favored few, for alas! the claimants were so many! Goethe himself, however, put the sign of his approval on the case of Corona Schroeter, not by putting her name in the mouths of scandal-mongers, but by embalming it in the verses which he wrote "On the death of Miedling." Miedling was an actor of the company which was wont to entertain the grand ducal court before the Court Theatre had been called into existence. So was Corona Schroeter, whom Goethe met first in Leipsic and brought to Weimar in 1778. She was then thirty years old, a singer, actress, composer of songs (she set some of Goethe's verses), and, in an amateur way, painter. The portrait which she gave to Goethe contrasts strongly with that of Jagemann in respect of spirituality, and would attract attention aside from its associations. I fear but little of the beauty of Goethe's tribute will appear in the following attempt at a translation of the lines which are devoted to this lovely woman in the poem referred to:

GOETHE AND LISZT

More room, my friends! Fall back a little space!
See one approach with bearing full of grace!
'T is she herself, on whom we e'er depend —
Our pray'rs are heard — their gift the muses send!
You know her well, the cause of sure delight,
A wondrous flower she bursts upon our sight.
To be a model she to earth was sent
Wherein the real and ideal should be blent.
Of all their gifts the nine withheld no part,
And nature breathed in her the breath of art.
To lend her charms the world itself is spent,
And e'en thy name, Corona, is an ornament.
Behold her now! Her movements light as air,
Unconscious she who seems with purpose fair!
In her observe with grateful, deep surprise,
An ideal mixture, saved for artists' eyes!

The collection of programmes in the Library reaching from 1793 down to date, and encompassing both periods of renown enjoyed by Weimar's Theatre, tempted me once to a comparative study for which I did not have sufficient time. Instead I sought to gain what light I could by noting the repertories of certain years, selected because of their chronological relation. These were, so far as the opera under Goethe's administration was concerned, first, the third year of the existence of the theatre as a Court Theatre, say from October, 1793, to the end of 1794. The operatic list within this time was not imposing. Interesting appeared the first performance of Martini's "Tree of Diana," on October 10, 1793. This is the opera of which Da Ponte wrote the libretto simultaneously with that of "Don Giovanni," if his extremely fantastical memoirs written in New York are to be credited. Another first performance was that of Mozart's "Magic Flute" on January 16, 1794. It became popular at once as frequent repetitions evidence.

These are the only operatic first productions falling within the time, but a performance of Mozart's "Entführung" on June 16, 1794, deserves to be noticed because of a note upon the house-bill: *Madame Weber wird in der Rolle der Constanze sich zu empfehlen die Ehre haben.* The Madame Weber who made her début in the Weimar opera on this occasion was the mother of the composer of "Euryanthe" and "Der Freischütz." Carl Maria von Weber was eight years old at the time. His mother remained a member of the company from June to September, 1794, but as her name does not appear on the house-bills after the occasion just noted, I fancy that she did not succeed. The composer's talent was inherited from his father, Major Franz Anton von Weber, a soldier who was so passionately fond of music that he carried his violin with him on his promenades. Finally, it is said, his devotion to music caused him to neglect his duties as an officer and he was discharged from the service. He retired to private life and finally became a professional musician. The mother of Carl Maria was his second wife. The archives of the Weimar Theatre contain several letters from him, in one of which he deplores that he ever left Weimar, having yielded to bad advice, and in another offers to sell the score of an opera composed by his young son, which showed great talent. The opera was "Silvana." The remainder of the operatic list during the year under consideration consisted of Mozart's "Figaro," Dalayrac's "The Two Savoyards," Grétry's "Richard, Cœur de Lion," Paisiello's "King Theodore in Venice," Cimarosa's "Die vereitelte Ranke," Anfossi's "Circe," "Das Sommerfest der Braminen," by Wenzel Mueller, Martini's "Cosa Rara" (which Mozart honored by a humorous quotation in "Don Giovanni"), and three of Dittersdorf's clever musical comedies.

This list is fairly representative of the activities of small theatres at the time. A study of the programmes of the year 1807, the middle of Goethe's term as Artistic

REFLECTIONS IN WEIMAR

Director of the Theatre, shows a great improvement. The performances are more frequent, the list more ambitious, the novelties more frequent, and the character of the works seems to indicate a most marked betterment of the interpreting forces. The chief novelties are Paër's "Camilla" (May 26), Salieri's "Palmira" (May 31), Méhul's "Treasure Diggers" (June 14), and Paër's "Die Wegelagerer" (December 19). The fact that every one of these operas has disappeared from the stage may set some one to reflecting on the peculiar mortality of operas, for Paër, Salieri and Méhul belonged to the great composers of their age. The other composers represented in the year's list were Cimarosa, Cherubini, Martini, Schenck, Della Maria, Gaveaux, Dittersdorf, Monsigny, Winter, Mozart and Wranitzky, whose "Oberon" was considered a wonderful romantic opera till Weber's came. In the last year of the Consulship of Goethe the engagement of a pair of Italian singers led to the performance of some of those singular pot-pourri operas, the music of which was put together more or less deftly by the conductors of those days. Another singular episode is the appearance on the list of Maggie Mitchell's "Fanchon" (with another woman in the titular rôle, however) for which Himmel had written the music. In this period falls the first production at Weimar of "Fidelio," which took place on September 4, 1816, the companion of the Grand Duke's hours of recreation being the *Leonore* of the occasion. I went no further than the programmes to learn what measure of success Beethoven's opera enjoyed. It was given five times in eight months. And Beethoven is set down as a "von" instead of a "van" on the programme. Besides Beethoven's the names of Weigl, Isouard, Benda, Boïeldieu, Spontini, appeared in company with most of those already mentioned. Then came the fatal 12th of April, 1817, and Jagemann's effective instrument — the poodle.

Goethe could not approve the action of the Grand Duke who opened his theatre to a poodle, and resigned. That was the end of the first period in the history of the theatre which made Weimar a stopping place in one of my musical pilgrimages. The second period, specifically musical, also ended with a resignation. This time the Jagemann appears to have been Madame Public Taste, though it still seems a mystery how after ten years of such training as Liszt gave the people of Weimar they could have been deaf to the beauties of Cornelius's "Barber of Bagdad." There is a comical juxtaposition in the circumstance that a career which began with a successful production of "Martha" as a novelty should have ended with a disastrous production of "The Barber." There is also, doubtless, a chapter of unwritten history somewhere which explains Liszt's withdrawal from the conduct of the opera at Weimar more satisfactorily than the current accounts. Herr Pohl has rendered unnecessary any detailed account of Liszt's activities as Court Conductor Extraordinary at Weimar; but I confess that the evidences of his labors surprised me. Never was the devotion of an artist to high ideals more quickly demonstrated, never was liberality of taste more generously displayed, never was a lofty ideal more deeply impressed upon the artistic activities of an institution than in the case of Liszt's career in Weimar. Scarcely is his presence announced, as the conductor of the new opera "Martha," before the evidences of his lofty strivings begin to accumulate. In two weeks the orchestral concerts begin, and soon the *entr'-actes* at the plays are filled with high class musical performances.

INDEX

INDEX

Accompanied recitative, 31.
"Achille," 11, 13, 32.
Achilles, 29.
Adams, Mrs. Mehitabel, 193.
Addison, 23, 33, 34, 35.
"Adriano in Siria," 32.
Albertarelli, singer, 77.
"Alceste," 26.
"Alcide," 32.
"Alcino," 22.
"Alessandro," 8, 9, 12, 32, 51.
"Alfonso and Estrella," 246.
Allegri, "Miserere," 184, 185.
Amorevoli, singer, 14, 40, 50.
Amphion Thebas, ego domum, 52.
Ancient Music, concerts of, 63, 72.
Anderson, Edward Henry, 177.
Anderson, Elbert Ellery, 177, 185.
Anderson, Henry James, 177.
"Andromaca," 9.
Anfossi, composer, 259.
"Antigone," 32.
Antis, bishop and composer, 79.
Appianino, singer, 14, 40, 49.
Apprentices in London, 76.
Araia, Francesco, singer, 13.
Archbishop of Salzburg, 138, 139.
Archbishop of London, anecdote of, 71.
Aria agitata, 36.

Aria cantabile, 35.
Aria d'agilita, 36.
Aria di bravura, 36.
Aria di mezzo carattere, 35.
Aria di note e parola, 36.
Aria di portamento, 35.
Aria di strepito, 36.
Aria infuriata, 36.
Aria parlante, 36.
"Ariodante," 22.
Ariosti, composer, 22.
"Armida," 30.
"Arminio," 22.
Arne, Dr., composer, 92.
Arnold, Dr., composer, 63, 77.
Arrigoni, Carlo, composer, 3, 14, 22, 27.
"Arsace," 27.
Artaria, music publisher, 229.
"Artaserse," 8, 9, 11, 21, 32, 53, 92.
"Atalanta," 22.
"Attilio," 32.

Babbi, singer, 14, 40, 49.
Bacchierotti, singer, 77.
Bach, generic name for Thuringian musicians, 131.
Bach, Johann Christian, "the English Bach," 97.
Bach, Johann, Ernst, 247.
Bach, Johann Sebastian, Spitta's life of, 192; "Well Tempered Clavichord," 203.

INDEX

Badini, poet, 77.
Bagnblese, singer, 13, 40.
Bangs, Francis, 4.
"Barber of Bagdad," 247, 262.
Barbieri, singer, 13, 40.
Barck, Miss, singer, 77.
Barrymore, Lord, 81.
Barthelemon, Mr., 64, 77, 83.
Barthelemon, Mrs., 77.
Barthelemon, Miss, 78.
Bassi, Luigi, singer, 159.
Bass singers in the eighteenth century, 41.
Baumgarten, composer in London, 77.
Baumgartner, conductor at Covent Garden, 86.
Bayreuth festivals, 116, 147.
Beethoven, Mrs. Carl van, 202, 204, 205, 206.
Beethoven, Caspar Anton Carl van, brother of the composer, 226.
Beethoven, Haus Verein, 221, 230.
Beethoven, Johann van, father of the composer, 219, 227.
Beethoven, Louis van, grandfather of the composer, 215, 219, 227.
Beethoven, Ludwig van, 58, 78, 131, 134, 144, 149, 161; anecdotes of, 196 *et seq.*; meets a friend from Bonn, 196; the kettledrums in the seventh symphony, 197; his favorite symphony, 196; the Kärnthnerthor orchestra, 197; Rust's anecdote, 198; Schindler's devotion, 198; Hozalka's anecdote, 198; appreciation of Mozart, 199, 208; his wine bill, 199; Salis's anecdote, 200; offers marriage to a singer, 200; meeting with Mähler, 200; his pianoforte playing, 201; the absent bassoon player, 201; anger at Prince Lobkowitz, 20; plays the "Well Tempered Clavichord," 203; disorder in his room, 203; death of, 204; courtesy to Himmel, 205; under arrest, 206; intercourse with Cipriani Potter, 208; opinion of Mozart and Handel, 208; appreciation of Cherubini, 208; admiration for England, 208; opinion of Moscheles, 209; uses a bootjack on his pianoforte, 209; antipathy to being overheard, 209; his deafness, 210, 226, 233; his biographer Thayer, 189 *et seq.*, 192, 212 *et seq.*; temperance at table, 209; birthplace, 213 *et seq.*; museum at Bonn, 203, 212 *et seq.*; monument at Bonn, 220; portraits of, 228; his "immortal beloved," 228; his mother, 223 *et seq.*; pianoforte, 231; ear trumpets, 231; position in musical history, 233 *et seq.*; "Fidelio," 197, 201, 210, 261; "Eroica" symphony, 196, 200, 238; C minor symphony, 197; seventh symphony, 197, 238; ninth symphony, 238; "Wellington's Victory," 208, 232; pianoforte concertos, C minor and E flat, 211.
Beaumarchais, 165.
Beckenkamp, Casper, painter, 227.

INDEX

"Begehre nicht ein Glück zu gross," 80.
Belderbusch, minister, 226.
Benda, composer, 77, 261.
"Benvenuto Cellini," 246.
"Berenice," 22.
Berger, Freiherr von, 125.
Berlioz, Hector, 74, 248.
Bernacchi, singing teacher, 42.
Bernasconi, Andrea, singer, 14, 25, 26.
Bernasconi, Antonia, singer, 26, 27.
Bertolli, singer, 14, 40.
Beyle, Henri, 66.
Bianchi, Bianca, singer, 154.
Billington, Mrs., 65, 66, 67, 77, 86.
Biswanger, Herr, 59.
Blake, Lady, 63.
Blake, Sir Patrick, 85.
Bland, Mrs., singer, 77.
Blumb, Mr., 78.
Boïeldieu, 261.
Bombet, L. A. C., pseudonym, 67.
Borghi, violinist, 78.
Born, Baroness, 198.
Brandt-Forster, Ella, singer, 144, 145, 154, 158.
Brassey, London banker, 83, 94.
Breuning family, 230.
Breuning, Dr. Gerhard von, 204, 206.
Breuning, Stephen von, 204.
Bright, E., 7.
Brignt, John, 8.
Bright, Richard, 7, 8.
British Nobility, opera of the, 21, 22.
Broschi, Carlo (Farinelli), 27.
Broschi, Riccardo, 14, 25, 27.
Brunswick, Countess, 228.

Buononcini, composer, 17, 19, 21, 22.
Burney, Dr. Charles, 24, 26, 27, 28, 30, 31, 33, 37, 46, 47, 50, 77, 194.
Burney, Mrs., pianist, 77.
Byrom, John, 19, 21.
Byron, Lord, 161.

CADENZA, sung by Farinelli, 52; by Tesi, 48.
Caffarelli, singer, 48, 50, 51.
Calcagni, singer in London, 77.
Calvesi, singer in London, 79.
Cambridge, University of, 85.
"Camilla," 260.
Campo, Marquis del, 79.
Capelletti, singer in London, 77.
Capua, 30.
Capuzinerberg, 138, 139.
Carestini, 8, 9, 11, 22, 40, 51.
Carter, composer in London, 77.
Carpani, "Le Haydine," 66.
Cary, Annie Louise, 4.
Casentini, singer in London, 79.
Caspar, Wenzelaus, Elector of Treves, 224.
Castelcicala, Prince de, 79.
Catherine II., of Russia, 24.
"Catone," 8, 9, 12, 27, 32.
Celestina, singer, 13, 40.
Celestini, singer, 77.
Ceneda, Bishop of, 164.
Charity Children, singing of, 73, 74.
Charles Augustus, Grand Duke of Weimar, 244, 248, 251, 253.
Cherubini, 208, 260.
Chesterfield, Lord, 54.
Choris, singer in London, 77.
Cimarosa, 259, 260.
"Circe," 259.

INDEX

"Ciro riconosciuto," 11, 32.
Claremont, Lord, 91.
Clarence, Duke of, 93.
Clemens Augustus, Elector of Cologne, 215, 224, 225.
Clement, violinist, 77, 78.
Clementi, 77.
"Clemenza di Tito," 8, 32.
Cleveland, Grover, President of the United States, 193.
Collóredo, Hieronymus, 150.
Columbia College, 174.
Composers in London, 77.
Concerts of Ancient Music, 63, 72.
"Contesa de' Numi," 10, 38.
Conti, Gioacchino, 50, (also see Giziello).
Contralto voice in the eighteenth century, 46.
Cornelius, Peter von, 247, 262.
Corri, Miss, 84.
"Cosi fan tutte," 146, 161.
Covent Garden Theatre, 86.
Cramer, J. B., 75.
Cramer, William, 63, 77, 78.
"Creation," The, 58.
Crouch, Mrs., singer in London, 77.
Cuzzoni, singer, 9, 12, 22, 40, 43, 44, 45, 50; her rivalry with Faustina, 43; Handel's threat, 44.

DALAYRAC, "The Two Savoyards," 259.
Danhauser, Joseph, sculptor, 230.
Da Ponte, Lorenzo, his aim in "Don Giovanni," 156; in New York, 159 *et seq.*; career of, 161 *et seq.*; not a poet laureate, 161; his grave unknown, 162; arrival in America, 163, 166; born a Jew, 164; indecent attack on, 169; arrival in New York, 171; business ventures of, 171; residences in New York, 173; becomes professor at Columbia College, 174; transactions with the College, 175, 179; death and burial of, 132, 160, 163, 184; appearance of, 185; autobiography of, 164; "Compendium," 167; "Frottola per far ridere," 180, 186; "Storia Americana," 181; "Tree of Diana," 181.
Da Ponte, Lorenzo, Bishop of Ceneda, 164.
Da Ponte, Lorenzo L., 171.
Dassie, artist in London, 91.
"Das Sommerfest der Braminen," 259.
Davide, singer, 77.
Davis, Signorina, singer, 77.
"Deidama," 21.
Deiters, Dr. H., 194.
De la Valle, Mrs., 79.
Della Maria, 260.
"Demetrio," 8, 30.
"Demofoonte," 9, 32.
Devonshire, Duchess of, 73.
"Didone," 12, 32, 71.
Dies, biographer of Haydn, 95, 99.
"Die Entführung aus dem Serail," 46, 258.
"Die vereitelte Ranke," 259.
"Die Wegelagerer," 260.
Dittenhoffer, composer in London, 77.
Dittersdorf, Carl Ditters von, 134, 259, 260.
Dobson, Austin, 3, 4, 6, 12, 15.

INDEX

Doctors of Music in London, 77.
"Dog of Aubri de Mont-Didier," the, 252, 254.
Dom Musikverein in Salzburg, 144.
"Don Carlos," 250.
"Don Giovanni," 143, 144, 149, 154, 155, 159, 161, 165, 178, 199, 250, 255, 258, 259.
Dorelli, singer in London, 77.
Dresden opera, 46, 50.
Dresden Tonkünstlerverein, 159.
Duprez, at the Charity Children's concert, 75.
Dupuis, Dr., 63, 77.
Durastanti, singer, 50.
Dussek, 77.

"Egeria," 33.
Egiziello (Giziello), 11.
Ende-Andriessen, 154.
England, national debt of, 62.
Eppinger, Dr. Joseph, 203.
Ernst Augustus, Grand Duke of Weimar, 247.
"Eroe," 32.
Essipoff, Madame, 146, 149.
Esterhazy, Prince, 86.
"Euryanthe," 258.
"Ezio," 29, 32.

"Fanchon," 260.
Farfallino, singer, 9, 40, 50.
Farinelli, singer, 8, 9, 12, 13, 14, 22, 27, 28, 34, 40, 43, 48, 49, 51, 52.
"Farnace," 12.
"Faust," Goethe's, 250.
Faustina, singer, 8, 9, 13, 28, 40, 43, 44, 45.
Felix, violinist in London, 78.
Felix, Benedikt, singer, 155.
Fénelon, 226.

Ferri, skill of, 34.
Fétis, 37, 97, 98.
"Fidelio," 78, 197, 201, 210, 261.
Fini, Michele, 12, 14, 25, 26.
Fischer, oboist in London, 78.
Fischer, Caecilia, 219.
Fischer, Gottfried, 219, 231.
Fleming, Marjorie, 97.
Forgery, now punished in England, 70.
Forster, Gustav, 130.
"For unto us," 64.
Fox, Charles James, 72.
Fox, Jabez, 194.
Fox, Mrs. Jabez, 195, 203.
Francesco, Carlo, 165.
Francis, Dr. J. W., 184, 186.
Frederickson, Charles W., 4, 8.
"Freischütz," 258.
Freny, Rudolf, opera singer, 154.
Friderici, composer in London, 77.
Frike, composer in London, 77.

Galuppi, 3, 14, 22, 23, 24, 26, 27, 31, 32.
Galvani and Beethoven, 200.
Game, prices of, in London, 72.
Garcia, Manuel, 177.
Gaveaux, 260.
"Genoveva," 246.
Genziger, Mrs., 59.
George I., King of England, 20.
German singers and Mozart's music, 155.
"Gerusalemme liberata," 30.
Giacomelli, 9, 25, 27.
Giaii, Antonio, 9, 13, 25.
Giardini, 71, 78.
Giornowichi, violinist in London, 78.

INDEX

Girowetz, composer in London, 77.
"Giustino," 22.
Giziello, singer, 11, 22, 40, 50, 51.
Gluck, 26, 32.
"God save the King," 91.
Goethe, 98, 134; his influence in Weimar, 243 *et seq.*; and Shakespeare, 249; quarrel with Herder, 251; episode with a poodle, 251, 261; admiration for Corona Schroeter, 255; "On the death of Miedling," 256.
"Gott im Herz," 80.
Graf, pianoforte maker, 231.
Graff, musician in London, 77, 78.
Gray, Thomas, his musical collection, 3 *et seq.*; his taste, 15; his singing, 17; as a harpsichord player, 17; interest in opera, 200.
Grétry, 259.
Grillparzer, recollections of Beethoven, 209; relations with Beethoven, 209.
Grosdill, violincellist in London, 77.
Grove, Sir George, dedication, 25, 27, 29, 97, 166, 202.
Guglielmi, "La Pastorella nobile," 79.
Guicciardi, Countess, 228.
Guildhall, 59.
Guttenbrun, painter in London, 91.
Guy Fawkes Day, 81.

"Hallelujah" chorus, 64, 83, 89.
Handel, 18, 19, 21, 22, 27, 29, 30, 42, 43, 50, 51, 76; his operatic ventures, 20 *et seq.*; and Cuzzoni, 44; and Tesi, 46; his bass singers, 41; Commemoration, 82, 83; admired by Beethoven, 208; "Jephtha," 18.
"Hannibal," 29, 30.
Hardy, painter in London, 91.
"Harmony in an Uproar," 27.
Harrington, oboist in London, 78.
Harrison, singer in London, 77.
Hartman, flautist in London, 79.
Hasse, Johann Adolf, 8, 9, 13, 17, 21, 28, 31, 32, 33, 41, 45, 48, 52, 53.
Hastings, Warren, 64.
Hauser, Anna, 155.
Haydn, in London, 55 *et seq.*; his note-books, 57 *et seq.*; "Creation," 58; his description of the Lord Mayor's dinner, 59; gifts for friends, 59; description of the races, 67; at Charity Children's concert, 73; his description of Vauxhall Gardens, 76; visits the Duke of York, 84; visits Cambridge University, 85; records Mozart's death, 87; describes Haymarket Theatre, 88; visits Oxford University, 88, 89; canon, "Thy Voice, O harmony," 89; bled in London, 89; visit to Mr. Shaw, 89; trip on the Thames, 89; concerts in London, 91; portraits of, 91; purchases for friends, 92; his English love, 95; love letters to, 95 *et seq.*;

INDEX

his wife, 96; tempo of his minuets, 149; his birth-place, 213; symphony in D, 84, 90; symphony in B flat, 90.
Haymarket Theatre in London, 20, 71, 88.
Hellmesberger Quartet, 146.
Herder, 244, 250, 251.
Herschel, Dr., 64.
Herzog, theatrical director in Vienna, 207.
Hess, Mus. Doc. in London, 77.
Heygendorf, Frau von, 253.
"Hide me from day's garish eye," 19.
Hillisbury, dancer in London, 79.
Himmel, composer, 205, 261.
Hindmarsh, violinist in London, 77.
Höfel, Blasius, 206, 229.
Hogarth on the opera of the eighteenth century, 35.
Hohensalzburg, 117.
Hoppner, painter in London, 91.
"How to listen to Music," 34.
Hozalka's anecdote of Beethoven, 198.
Hüllmandl, composer in London, 77, 78.
Hüttenbrenner, Anselm, his account of Beethoven's death, 203.
Hummel, J. F., 125, 144, 145, 155.
Hummel, J. N., 78, 213.
Hungarian Gypsy bands, 11.
Hunter, surgeon in London, 62.
"Hydaspes," 33.

IMAGINATION, Ruskin on the, 239.

"Io vi mando questo foglio," 75.
"Ipermestra," 32.
"Iphigenia," 250.
Isouard, 261.
"Issipile," 8.
Italian basses, lack of, 42.

JAGEMANN, Fräulein, 252, 261.
Jahn, Otto, 192.
Jahn, Wilhelm, 120, 143, 148, 158.
Jansa, Miss, pianist in London, 78.
Jarowez, violinist in London, 78.
"Jephtha," 18.
Joachim, Joseph, 223.
Jomelli, 31.
Jones's Chant, 74.
Jordan, Dora, 93.
Joseph Clemens, Elector of Cologne, 215, 225.
Joseph II., of Austria, 165, 181.

KAULICH, Louise, singer, 144, 154.
Kees, Mr. and Mrs. von, 59, 92.
Kelly, Michael, 63, 64, 66, 77, 187.
"Kenne Gott," a canon, 80.
Kettledrummer, anecdote of, 72.
Keverich, Maria Magdalena, 227.
"King Alfred," 246.
"King of Arragon," 27.
"King Theodore in Venice," 259.
King's Theatre, London, 20, 21.
Klein, Franz, sculptor, 229.
Kranz, conductor in Weimar, 255.
Krenn, musikdirektor, 196.

271

INDEX

Krolop, Franz, singer, 154.
Krumpholz and wife, 78, 79.
Küffner, Hofrath, 196.
Kuppe, William, 221.

LABORDE, 26.
"Lacrymosa," 125, 126.
Lampugnani, 13, 15, 22, 25, 27.
Latilla, 9, 15, 24, 25, 26.
La Trobe, composer in London, 77.
Latronne, painter, 229.
Laym, Johann, 227.
Lazarini, singer in London, 77, 79.
Leeds, Duke of, 59.
Lehmann, Marie and Lilli, 154.
Lenné, Peter, 196.
Lenz, pianist in London, 78.
Leo, Leonardo, 11, 16, 17, 28, 32.
Leopold, Emperor of Austria, 166.
Lichnowsky, Prince, 78.
Ligi, Celestino, 14, 27.
Lincoln, Abraham, President of the United States, 193.
Lincoln's Inn Fields, 21.
Linnæus, "Systema Naturæ," 3.
Liszt, his influence in Weimar, 243 *et seq.*
Livington family, 174.
Lobkowitz, Prince, Beethoven's friend, 201.
Lockhart, 75.
"Lohengrin," 246.
Lolli, oboist in London, 78.
London, composers in, 77; consumption of coal by, 70; Doctors of Music in, 77; fog, 93; houses built in, 70-81; deaths in, in 1791, 75; oboists in, 78; pianists in, 77, 78; singers in, 77; street-cleaning, 89; violinists in, 77, 78; violoncellists in, 77; Lord Mayor's dinner, 59.
Lops, singer in London, 77.
Lorenzino, 40, 50.
Louis, Dauphin of France, 10.
Louis XV., of France, 10.
Louis XVI., of France, 10.
Lully, his overture form, 11.
Lyser, portrait of Beethoven, 231.

MACAULAY, 235.
Macneven, Dr., 184, 185.
Maelzel, 231, 233.
Maffei, singer in London, 77, 78.
"Magic Flute," 116, 138, 144, 145, 153, 199, 258.
Mähler, J. W., 200, 201, 231.
Male sopranos and contraltos, 42.
Malibran, 177.
Manzuoli, Giovanni, 14, 40, 49.
Mara, 'cellist, 63, 77.
Mara, Madame, 63, 71, 77, 89.
Marcello, Benedetto, 16.
Marchesi, Signor, 82.
Marchetti, 23.
Maria Theresa, 214.
Marie Antoinette, 166.
Marionet Theatre, 91.
Marlborough, Duke of, 225.
Maroncelli, 185.
Marriage customs in London, 85.
"Marriage of Figaro," 120, 125, 142, 143, 150, 154, 155, 156, 157, 161, 187, 259.
"Martha," 262.
Martini, 181, 258, 259, 260.
Mason, Lowell, 193.

INDEX

Mason, the Rev. William, 7, 16, 18, 19.
Mayer, Frederike, singer, 146.
Mazini, composer, 77.
Mazzanti, singer in London, 77.
Mazzoni, composer, 14, 25.
Méhul, "The Treasure Diggers," 260.
Mendel's German Lexicon, 31.
Mendelssohn, 149.
Menel, 'cellist in London, 77.
"Messiah," The, 64.
Metastasio, poet, 10, 32, 33, 36.
Meyerbeer, 32.
Michelangelo, 245.
Milk, how preserved, 83.
Mingotti, 28.
Minuets at Lord Mayor's dinner, 60.
Minuet, tempo of, 149.
Mitchell, Maggie, American actress, 260.
Mitford, the Rev. John, 16, 18.
"Mitridate," 26.
Mönchsberg, the, 139.
Monsigny, 260.
Montagnana, 22.
Montagu, Lady Mary Wortley, 54.
Monticelli, 12, 40, 51.
Montressor, 178.
Moore, Clement Clarke, 174, 180, 185.
Moravian clergyman, anecdote of, 71.
Morelli, singer, 77.
Moscheles, Beethoven's opinion of, 209.
Motley, John Lothrop, 193.
Motzert family, 129.
Mozart, Carl, 129.
Mozart, Leopold, 136, 139.
Mozart, Marie Anna, 130.
Mozart, Wolfgang Amadeus, 26, 32; and Manzuoli, 49; parting with Haydn, 87; centenary of his death, 113 *et seq.*; music at, 142; birth-place, 119, 136; death and burial of, 87, 125, 131, 160, 184; his music slowly appreciated, 134; relics of, at Salzburg, 134; his poverty, 135; his clavichord and pianoforte, 135, 136; his "Wohnhaus," 139; domestic life, 128; descendants of, 128; widow, 130, 132; Beethoven's appreciation, 198, 199, 208; Viennese performances of his music, 146; the spirit of his music, 148; German singers and his music, 155; Jahn's biography, 192; his operas in Weimar, 250, 254, 260; "Requiem," 116, 118, 121, 125, 126, 142, 143, 144, 145, 153; "Jupiter" symphony, 143, 146, 148, 149; G minor symphony, 143, 148; operas, see "Cosi fan tutte," "Die Entführung," "Don Giovanni," "Marriage of Figaro," and "Magic Flute;" pianoforte concerto in D minor, 146, 149; quartet in D minor, 146; quintet in G minor, 146; "Bundeslied," 141; "Vergiss Mein Nicht," 146; "Das Veilchen," 146; "O Isis," 146; *Pamina's* air, 146; "Dies Bildniss," 146; "In diesen heil'gen Hallen," 146; "Wiegenlied," 146; "Porge amor," 155.
Mozart, W. A., son, 128, 129.

INDEX

Mozarteum in Salzburg, 115, 144, 145, 155.
Mueller, Wenzel, "Das Sommerfest," 259.
Murder, how punished in London, 70.
Music, its relationship to the other arts, 235.
Musical tradition, 147.
Musico, the, 42.

NAPOLEON BONAPARTE, 161, 180.
Neate, Charles, and Beethoven, 230.
Neesen, portrait of Beethoven, 210, 211.
Negri, singer in London, 77.
Nicolai, Royal Chamberlain and composer, 79.
Nicolini, singer, 33, 34.
Nissen, G. N. von, 130, 132, 137.
"Nitetti," 32.
Nobilita Britannica, opera of, 21, 22.
"No more to Ammon's God," 18.
Noyan, a drink, 93.

OATLANDS, Castle, 84.
"Oberon," 260.
Oboists in London, 78.
Old Hundredth Psalm, 75.
"Olimpiade," 11, 12, 13, 32.
Opera, artificiality of, 35.
Operatic formula in the eighteenth century, 36.
Operatic lovers, 42.
Operatic singing in the eighteenth century, 34.
Oranges from Portugal, 93.
Orlandini, 13, 14, 25.

"Orlando Furioso," 30.
Ott, painter in London, 81, 91.
Oulibischeff, 163.
Oxford, University of, 85.

PAGET, Violet, 23.
Paër, Ferdinand, 260.
Paisiello, 259.
Palestrina, 16, 18.
"Palmira," 260.
Pantheon Theatre, burned, 70.
"Partenope," 33.
"Pastorella nobile," 79.
Pellico, 185.
Pembroke, Countess, 45.
Perez, David, 9, 15, 29.
Pergolese, 3, 9, 12, 13, 16, 28, 51.
"Per questo dolce amplesso," 53.
Pertici, 26.
Peterborough, Lord and Lady, 54.
Petrarch, 174, 179.
Philharmonic Society of Vienna, 120, 124, 143, 147.
Philip V., of Spain, 53.
Pianists in London, 77, 78.
Piccini, 26, 31.
Pistocchi, 42.
Pitt, Prime Minister, 59, 61.
Pleyel, Ignaz, 79, 88.
Pohl, C. F., 57, 58, 63, 67, 84, 95.
Pohl, R., 262.
Polignac, Marquis de, 10.
Pool, Miss, singer in London, 77.
Porpora, 21, 22, 42.
Potter, Cipriani, and Beethoven, 208.
Prescott, W. H., 174.
Price, Mr., 18.

INDEX

Prince of Wales, 82, 84.
Professional concerts, 72, 76, 88.
Punch, Prince of Wales's, 82.
Purcell, 72.

QUAKERS and the king's tax, 82.
Queen's Theatre, 20.

RAFF, Joachim, "King Alfred," 246.
Raimondi, violinist in London, 78.
Raymond, Mrs. C. M., 4.
Recitative, accompanied, 31.
Rees's Encyclopædia, 97, 98.
Regole per l'accompagnamento, 3, 12.
Reichenberg, Franz, singer, 144, 146.
Reichmann, Theodor, 154.
Reimschneider, bass, 41, 42.
Reinhold, bass, 41.
"Re pastore," 32.
Reynolds, Sir Joshua, 66, 67.
"Richard, Cœur de Lion," 259.
Richter, Hans, 154.
Ries, Ferdinand, 196.
"Rinaldo," 30, 34.
Rinaldo di Capua, 14, 28, 29, 30, 37.
Ritter, F. L., 167.
Ritter, Josef, singer, 145, 154.
Rivafinoli, opera manager in New York, 178.
"Robbers," The, 250.
Robinson, Anastasia, singer, 54.
"Rodelinda," 12, 44.
"Romolo ed Ersilio," 33.
Roschi, basso, 41.
Rossi, librettist, 32.
Rossini, 32, 134, 156, 157.
Royal Society of Musicians, 63.

"Ruggiero," 33.
Ruskin, John, 3, 239.
Rust, Wilhelm, 198.

SACCHINI, 31.
Saint Peter, picture of, 71.
Salieri, 134, 165, 181; "Palmira," 260.
Salis, anecdote of Beethoven, 200.
Salomon, 72, 76, 77, 87, 88, 91.
Salterio, 11.
Salzach, the, 139.
Salzburg, 115, 118, 136; Liedertafel, 146; description of, 137; Royal Imperial Theatre, 150.
Sarro, Domenico, 13, 25, 32.
Sarti, 71.
Sassarelli, singer, 34.
Sassone, il (Hasse), 8, 9, 13, 28.
Scalzi, singer, 12, 40, 50.
Scarlatti, A., 31.
Scarlatti, D., 17, 22.
Scheener, violinist in London, 78.
Schenck, 260.
Schiassi, Yaetano, 14, 25, 27.
Schiller, 204, 244, 245, 254.
Schindler, Anton, 204, 209.
Schinotti, singer in London, 77.
Schmidt, Victor, 155.
Schnittenhelm, Anton, 155.
Schroeter, Corona Elizabeth Wilhelmine, 98, 255.
Schroeter, Johann Heinrich, 98.
Schroeter, Johann Samuel, 97.
Schroeter, Mistress, 62; love letters to Haydn, 95 et seq.
Schubert, Franz, 161; "Alfonso and Estrella," 246.
Schumann, R., "Genoveva," 246.
Schwanthaler, sculptor, 128, 131.

INDEX

Scott, Sir Walter, 97, 161.
Scramb, 'cellist in London, 77.
Seconda, singer in London, 77, 78.
Selitti, composer, 14, 25.
"Semiramide," 9, 32.
Senesino, singer, 9, 13, 22, 34, 40, 43, 51, 54.
Serra, violinist in London, 78.
Sex in singers, 41.
Seyfried, Ignaz von, 197.
Shaw, Mr., visited by Haydn, 89.
Shield, composer in London, 77.
"Siface," 32.
"Silvana," 259.
Silvester, advocate and alderman, 59.
Silvester Chamberlain, 63.
Simoni, singer in London, 77.
Singers in London, 77.
Singers of the eighteenth century, 40 *et seq.*
"Siroë," 8, 9, 12.
Sonnenburg, Baroness von, 130.
Sontag, Henrietta, 249.
Sperati, 'cellist in London, 77.
Spitta, Philipp, "Life of Bach," 192.
"Sponsali d'Enea," 26.
Spontini, 261.
"Stabat Mater," 12.
Stadion, Count de, 79.
Stanhope, Lord, 54.
Staudigl, Jos., singer, 154.
Steele, R., 23, 33.
Stein, pianoforte maker, 209.
Stonehewer, Richard, 7, 8.
Storace, 63, 77.
Strada, singer, 11, 14, 22, 40, 43.
Strauss, Richard, 25.
Sumner, Charles, senator, 193.

Süssmayr, 126.
Swift, Dean, 19.

"Tasso," 250.
Taylor, opera manager in London, 166.
Telscher, artist, 204.
"Temistocle," 12, 13, 33.
Tenor singers, 41.
Tesi, singer, 8, 11, 12, 13, 40, 43, 46 *et seq.*
Thayer, Alexander W., 58; 191 *et seq.*; birth, 192; graduation, 192; with United States Legation in Vienna, 193; appointed Consul at Trieste, 193; member of the staff of the "New York Tribune," 193; works in the library of Harvard College, 193; catalogues Lowell Mason's library, 193; removed from consulship, 194; "Chronologisches Verzeichniss," 194; his notebooks, 195 *et seq.*; biography of Beethoven, 202, 212.
Theft, how punished in England, 70.
Tipping, in Austria, 123.
"Tito Manlio," 12.
Tomich, composer in London, 77.
"Treasure Diggers," 260.
"Tree of Diana," 258.
"Trionfo di Clelia," 33.
Tuckerman, H. T., 166, 184, 186.
Turcotti, singer, 12, 14. 40.
Twain, Mark, 244.
"'T was the Night Before Christmas," 174.

"Una Cosarara," 259.

INDEX

VAUXHALL, 76.
Veracini, composer, 22.
Verdi, 23.
Verein Beethoven-Haus, 221, 230.
Verplanck, Giulain C., 184, 185.
Viardot-Garcia, 159.
Vienna, Mozart's music in, 146.
Vinci, Leonardo, 9, 17, 22, 29, 32, 37.
Vinci, Leonardo da, 37; "Didone abbandonata," 39.
"Viol de gamboys," 38.
Violinists in London, 77, 78.
Violoncellists in London, 77.
Viscontina, singer, 12, 40.
Vogler, Johann Casper, 248.
"Vologeso," 30.

WAGNER, Richard, 147, 154; festival in Bayreuth, 116; on minuet tempo, 149; "Lohengrin," 246.
Waldendorf, Baroness, 224.
Wales, Prince of, 68, 82, 84.
Walpole, Horace, 3, 15, 18, 21, 24.
Walpole, Sir Robert, 45.
Walter, Gustav, singer, 144, 146.
Waltz, basso, 41.
Ward, Samuel, 185, 186.
Weber, Carl Maria von, mother of, 258; "Freischütz," 258;
"Euryanthe," 258; "Silvana," 259; "Oberon," 260.
Weber, Franz Anton von, 258.
Wegeler, Dr. F. G., 196, 217, 218, 219, 220, 229.
Weigl, Joseph, 57, 134, 181, 261.
Weimar, Grand Ducal Theatre, 134, 247; Reflections in, 241 et seq.; theatre and opera in, 245 et seq.
"Wer mit Vernunft betracht'," 80.
Wieland, 244.
William II., German Emperor, 232.
Willmann, singer, and Beethoven, 200.
Wilson, William, United States Senator, 193.
Wilt, Marie, singer, 124, 146, 154.
Windsor Chapel, 91.
"Woodman, The," 86.
"Worthy is the Lamb," 64.
Wranitzky, "Oberon," 260.

YORK, Duchess of, 63, 82, 84.
York, Duke of, 84.

ZAMPERELLI, Dionigi, 3, 14, 25.
Zeno, Apostolo, 32.
"Zingara," 31.

www.ingramcontent.com/pod-product-compliance
Lightning Source LLC
Chambersburg PA
CBHW032110230426
43672CB00009B/1695